0500000908675 7

CLICK: A STORY OF CYBERBULLYING

© 2018 Zuiker Press

Alexandra Philips Photographs © 2018 Alexandra Philips

Written by Anthony E. Zuiker
Art by Nam Kim and Garry Leach
Colors by Fahriza Kamaputra
Lettering by Jimmy Betancourt for Comicraft
Designed by Roberta Melzl
Edited by Dave Elliott

Founders: Michelle & Anthony E. Zuiker
Publisher: Sven Larsen

Published by Zuiker Press
16255 Ventura Blvd.
Suite #900
Encino, CA 91436
United States of America

Publicity by Jonalyn Morris PR
jonalyn@jonalynmorrispr.com and info@zuikerpress.com

Visit us online at www.zuikerpress.com

Library of Congress Catalog-in-Publication data is
available upon request.
ISBN 978-1-947378-04-9 (hardcover)

PRINTED IN CANADA
November 2018
10 9 8 7 6 5 4 3 2

DEDICATED TO ... every young person who needs to be reminded they are not alone.

HOPE lies within these pages.

ZUIKER PRESS

... is a husband and wife publishing company that champions the voices of young authors. We are an **ISSUE-BASED** literary house. All of our authors have elected to tell their personal stories and be the ambassadors of their cause. Their goal, as is ours, is that young people will learn from the pain and heroics of our authors and find **HOPE**, **HAPPINESS** and **CHANGE** in their own lives.

TEACHER'S CORNER

SHANNON LIVELY

is an educator with a bachelor's degree in elementary education from the University of Nevada, Las Vegas, and a master's degree from Southern Utah University, as well as advanced degrees in differentiated instruction and technology. In 2013, she was awarded the Barrick Gold One Classroom at a Time grant, then chosen as Teacher of the Year. She is currently completing the National Board Certification while teaching fifth grade at John C. Vanderburg Elementary School in Henderson, Nevada.

WHY WE HONOR TEACHERS

We understand the hard work it takes to be a teacher! It takes a lot of time to prepare work for students. At Zuiker Press, we want to give teachers access to class work with each book we publish. We will have a **TEACHER'S CORNER** area on our website, Zuikerpress.com, which will give teachers class work beyond the story. This is where you can partake in discussions, comprehension, reading groups, and other activities with your students. All of these printable resources will be under the umbrella of Common Core to stay consistent with how subjects are being taught. We hope this helps teachers utilize each story to the fullest extent!

5

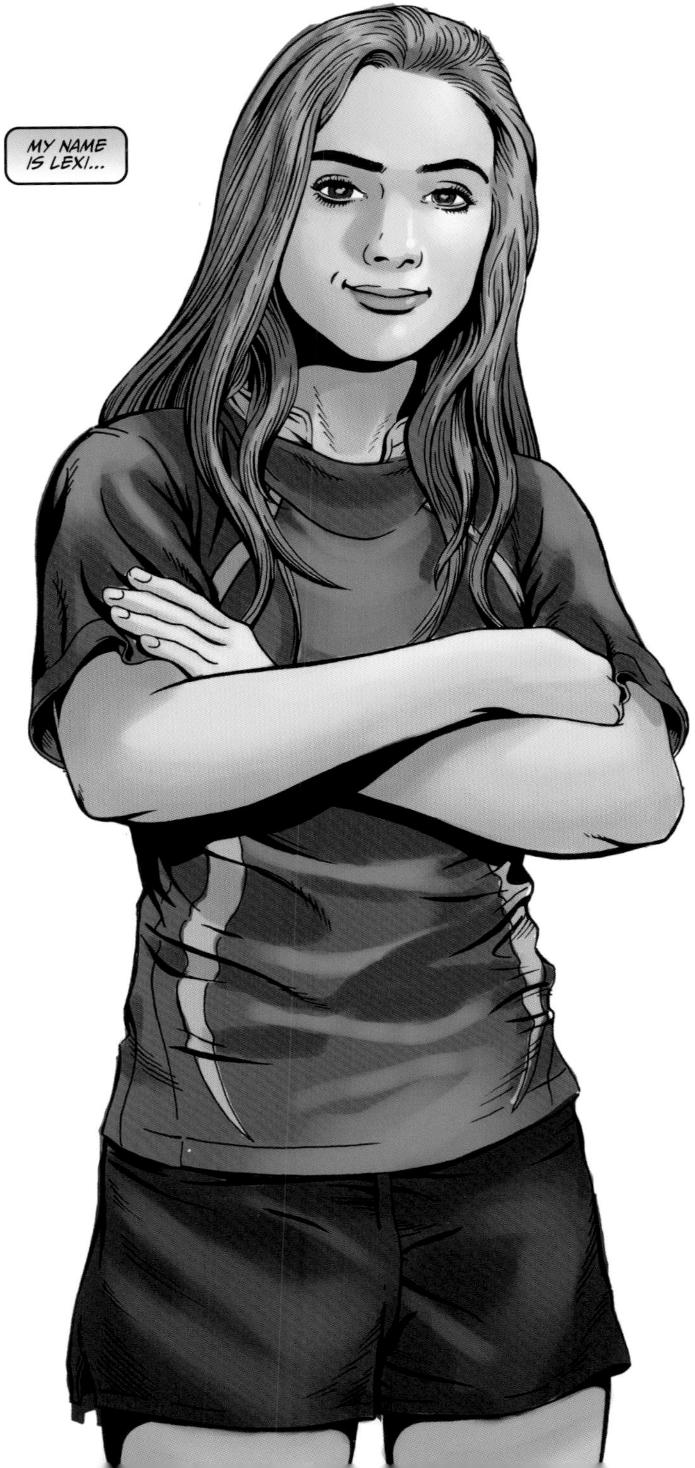
MY NAME IS LEXI...

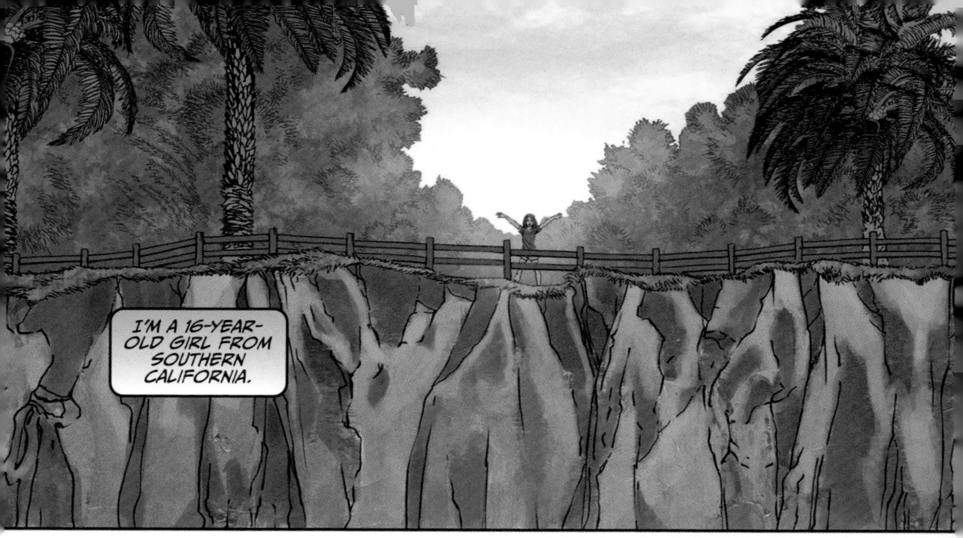
I'M A 16-YEAR-OLD GIRL FROM SOUTHERN CALIFORNIA.

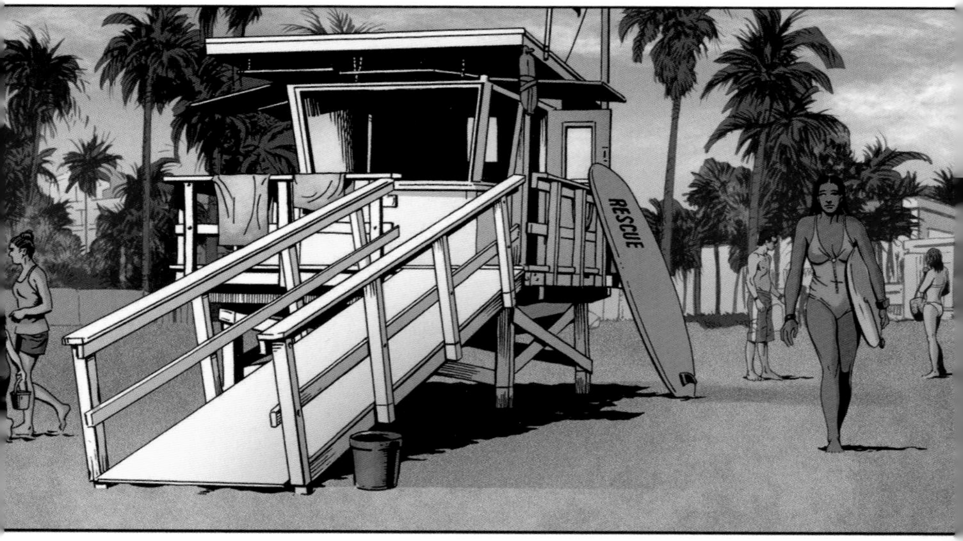
RESCUE

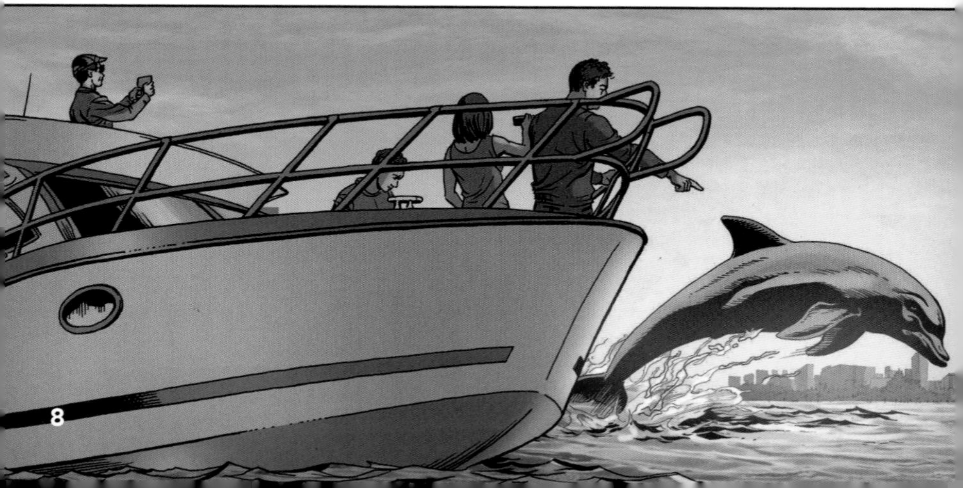

THIS YEAR I'M HAPPY TO SAY, I AM GOING INTO ELEVENTH GRADE. A JUNIOR IN HIGH SCHOOL.

FOR MOST KIDS MY AGE, IT'S NOT THAT BIG A DEAL.

BUT FOR ME, IT IS A BIG DEAL...

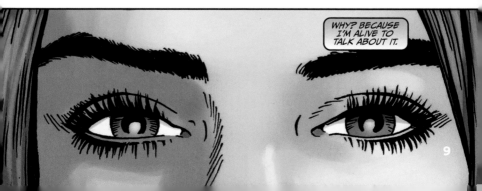

WHY? BECAUSE I'M ALIVE TO TALK ABOUT IT.

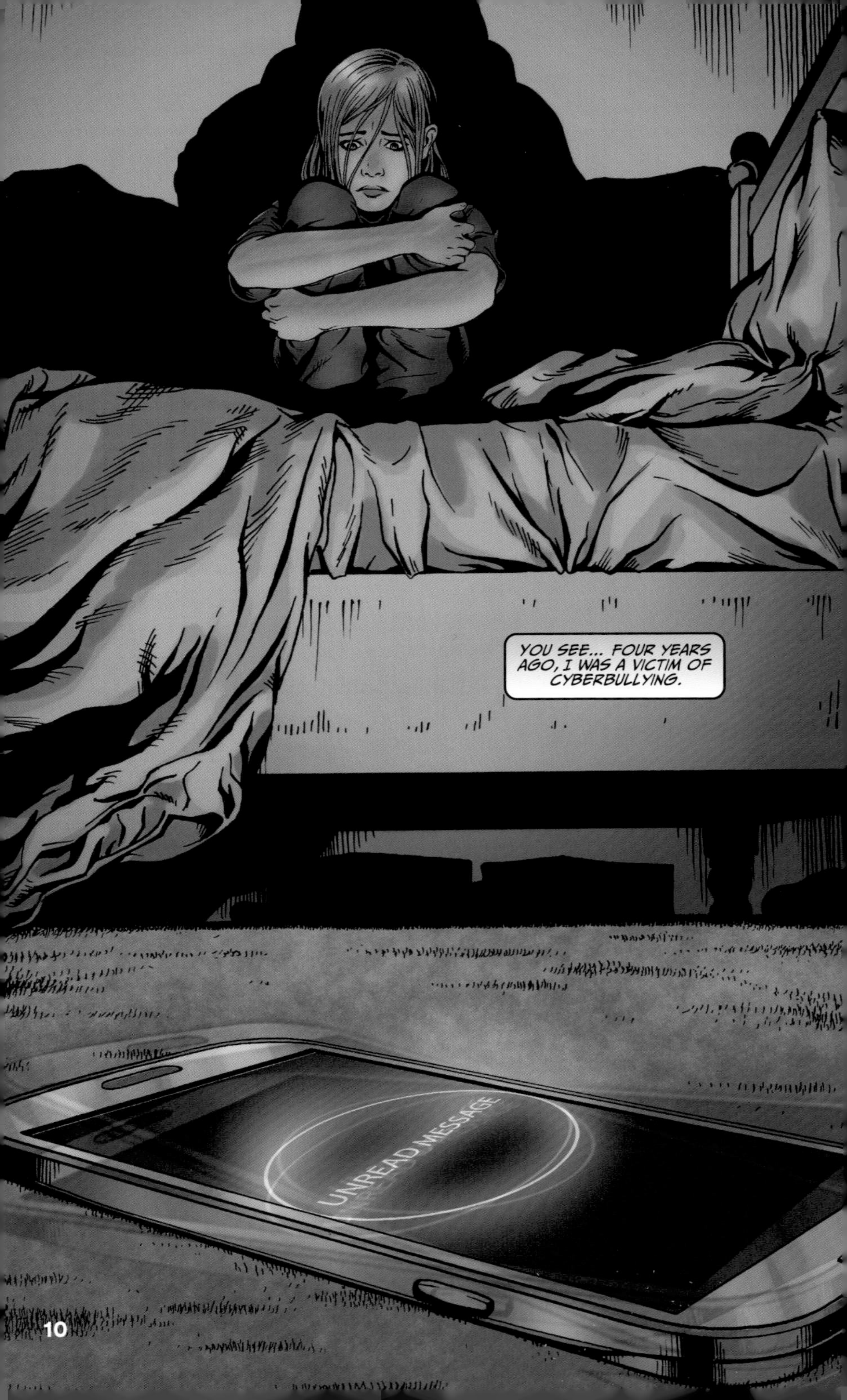
YOU SEE... FOUR YEARS AGO, I WAS A VICTIM OF CYBERBULLYING.
UNREAD MESSAGE

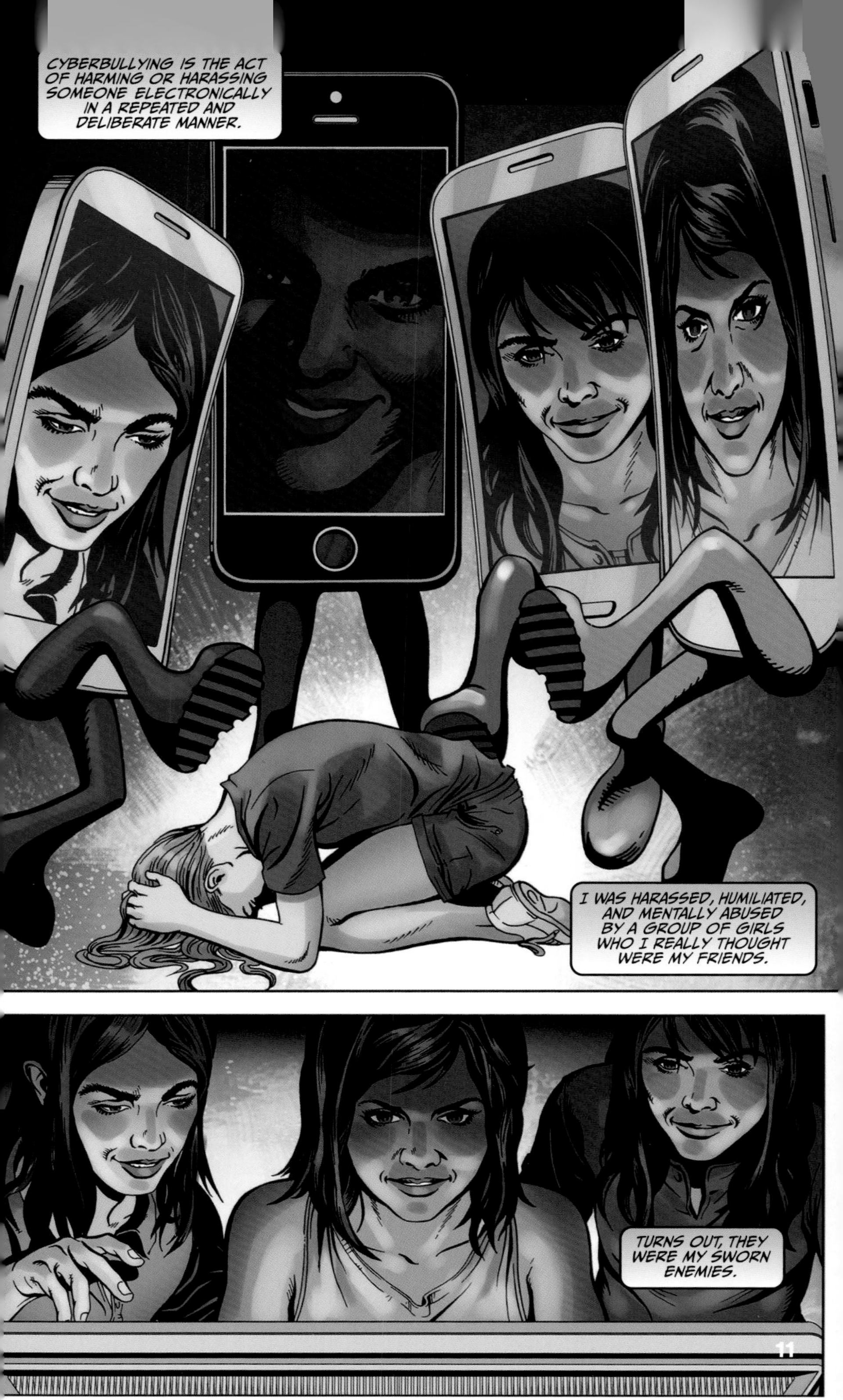
CYBERBULLYING IS THE ACT OF HARMING OR HARASSING SOMEONE ELECTRONICALLY IN A REPEATED AND DELIBERATE MANNER.
I WAS HARASSED, HUMILIATED, AND MENTALLY ABUSED BY A GROUP OF GIRLS WHO I REALLY THOUGHT WERE MY FRIENDS.
TURNS OUT, THEY WERE MY SWORN ENEMIES.

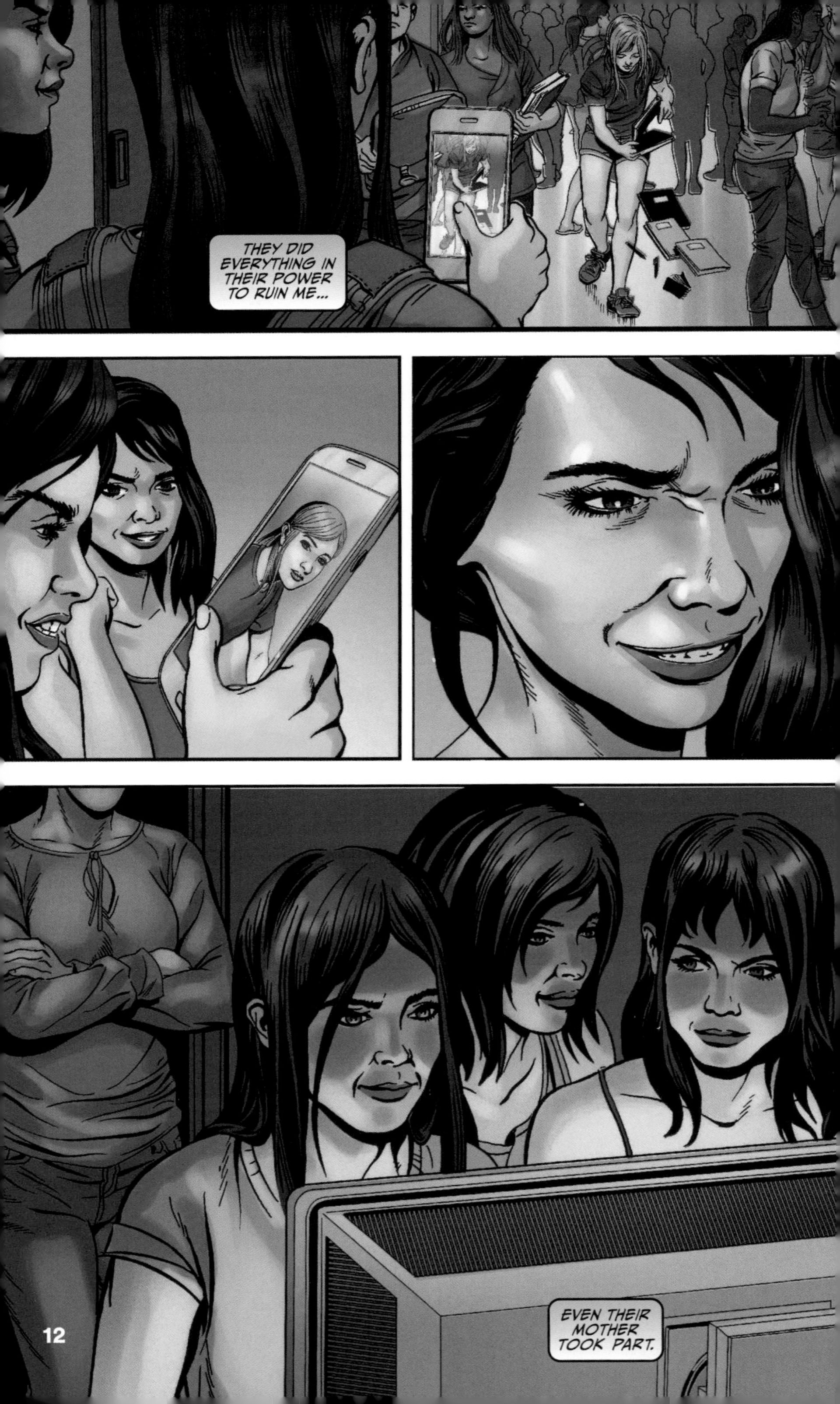
THEY DID EVERYTHING IN THEIR POWER TO RUIN ME...
EVEN THEIR MOTHER TOOK PART.

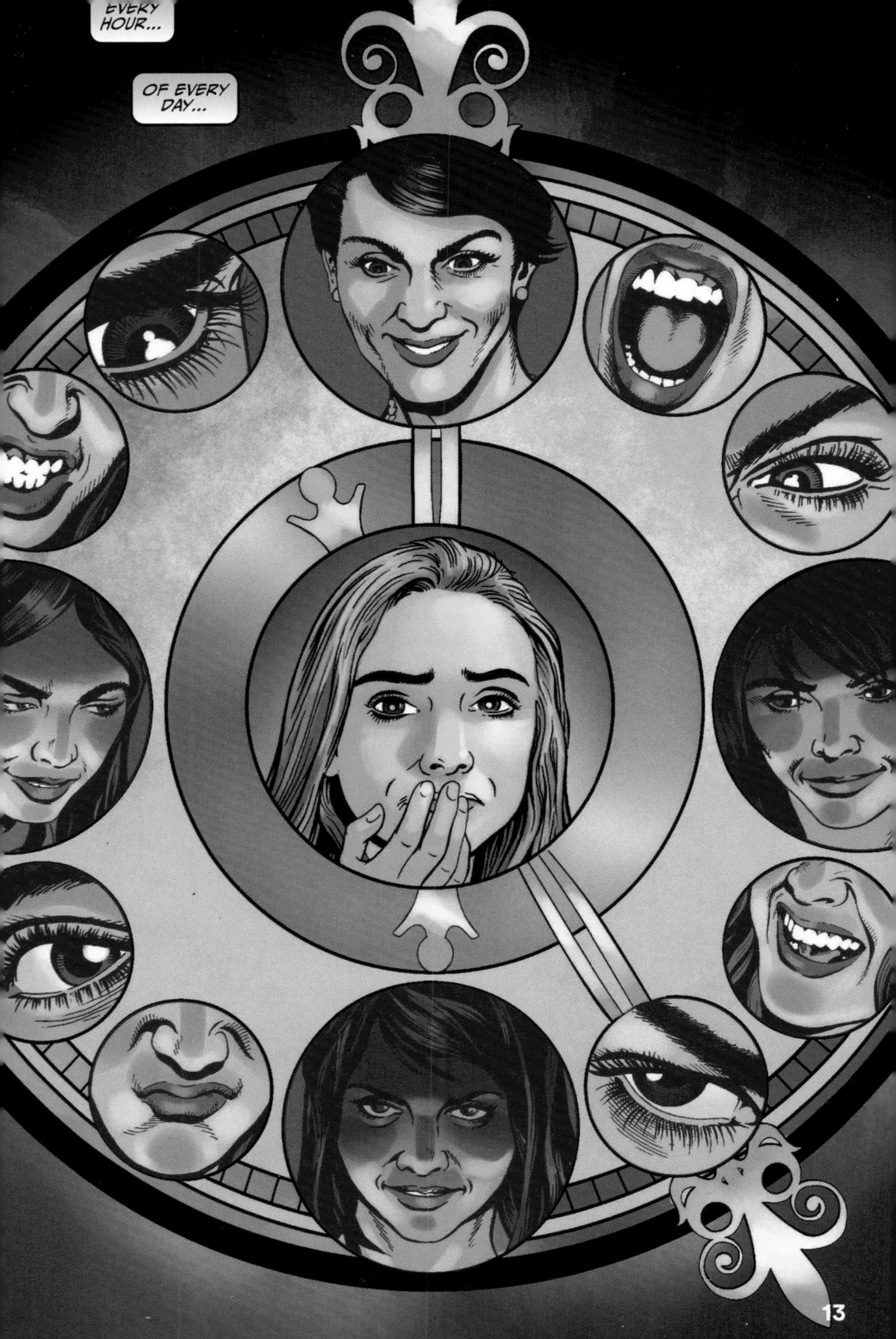
EVERY HOUR...
OF EVERY DAY...

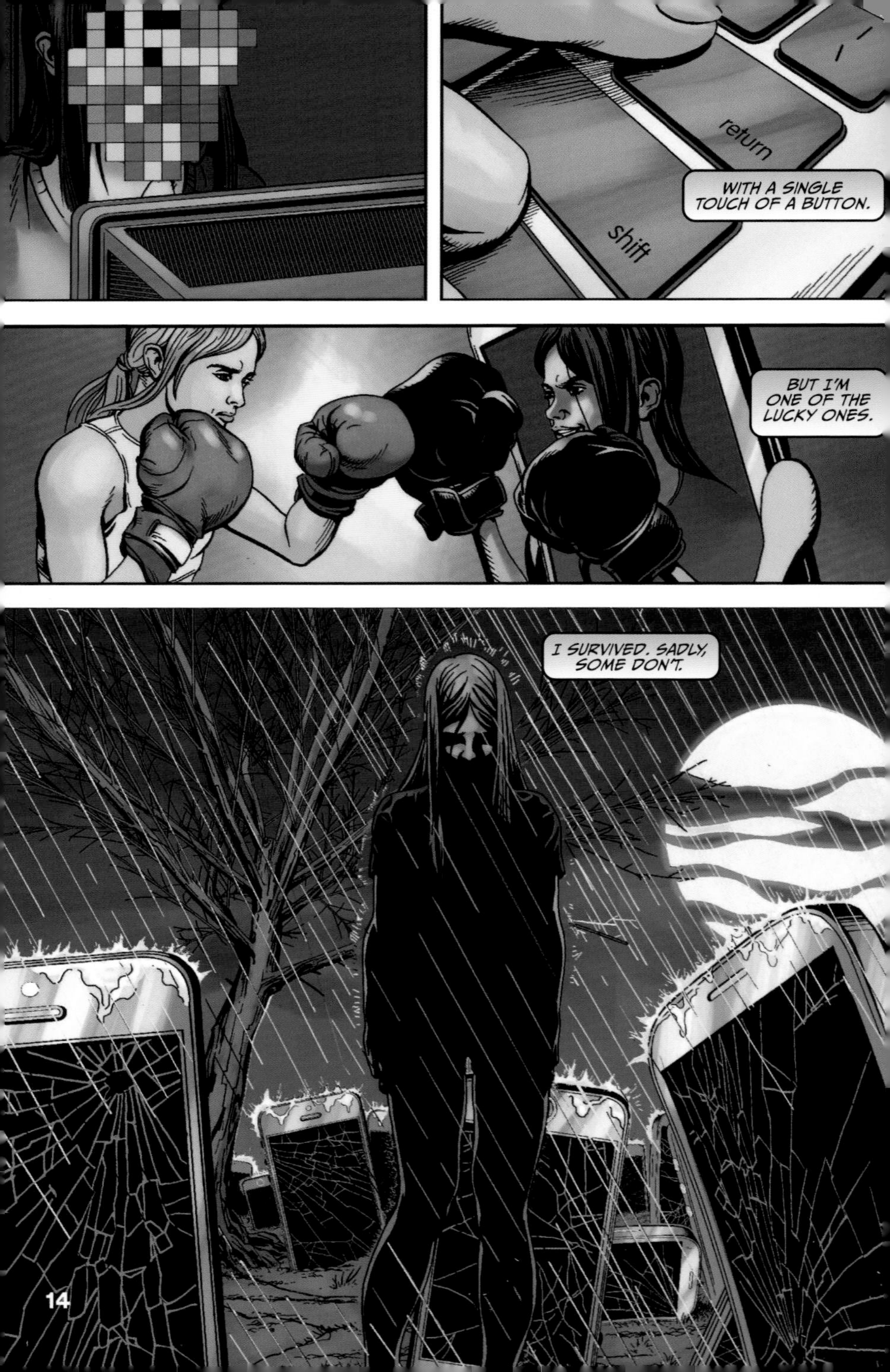
return
shift
WITH A SINGLE TOUCH OF A BUTTON.
BUT I'M ONE OF THE LUCKY ONES.
I SURVIVED. SADLY, SOME DON'T.

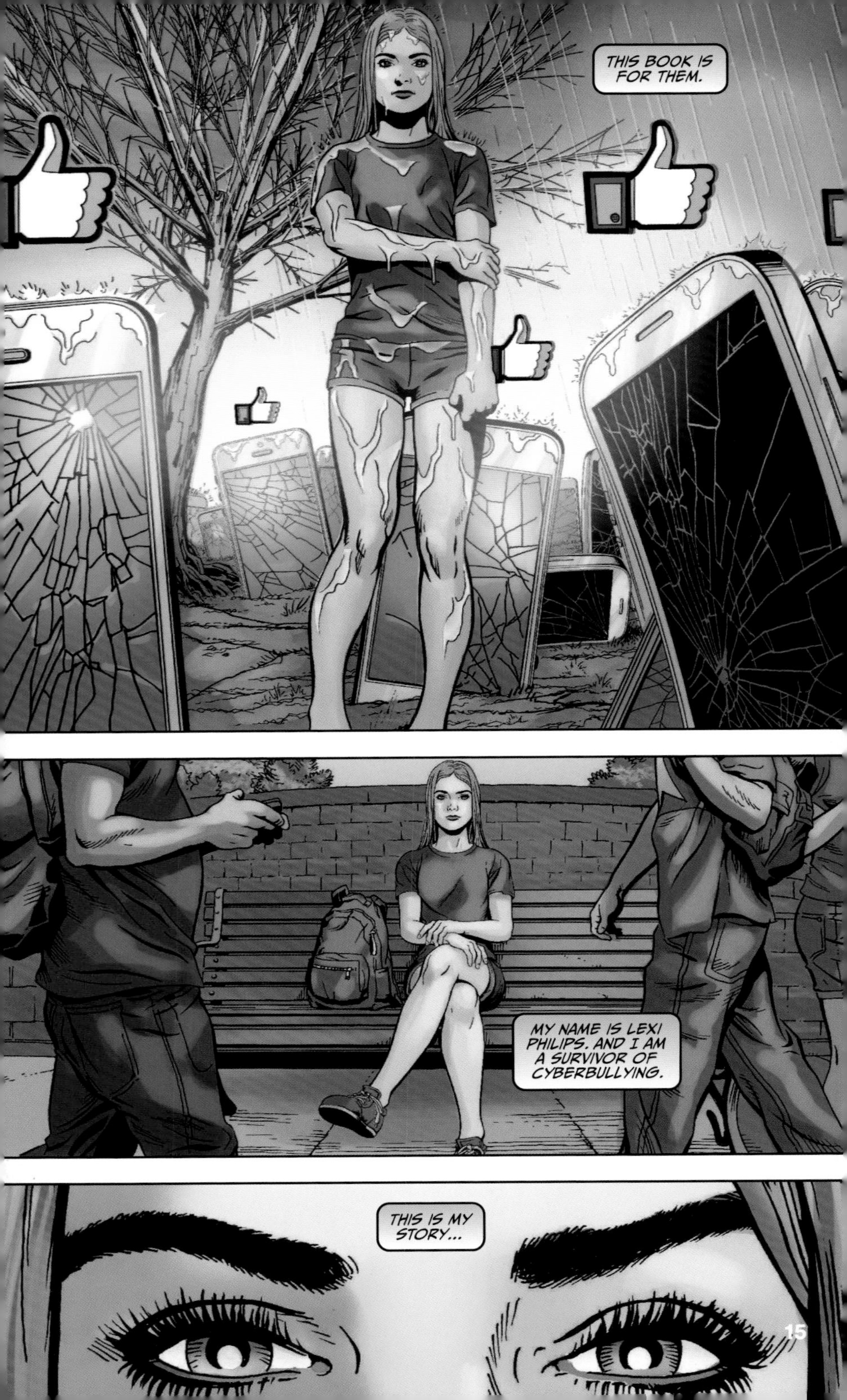
THIS BOOK IS FOR THEM.
MY NAME IS LEXI PHILIPS. AND I AM A SURVIVOR OF CYBERBULLYING.
THIS IS MY STORY...

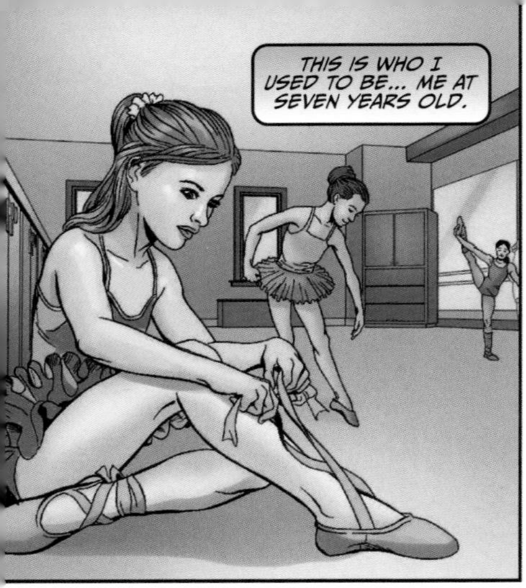
THIS IS WHO I USED TO BE... ME AT SEVEN YEARS OLD.

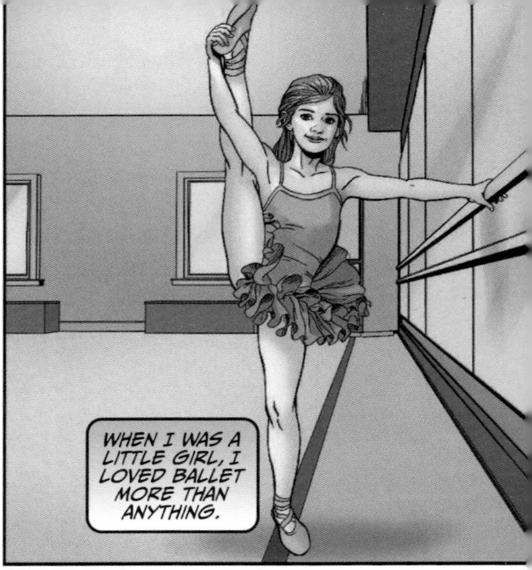
WHEN I WAS A LITTLE GIRL, I LOVED BALLET MORE THAN ANYTHING.

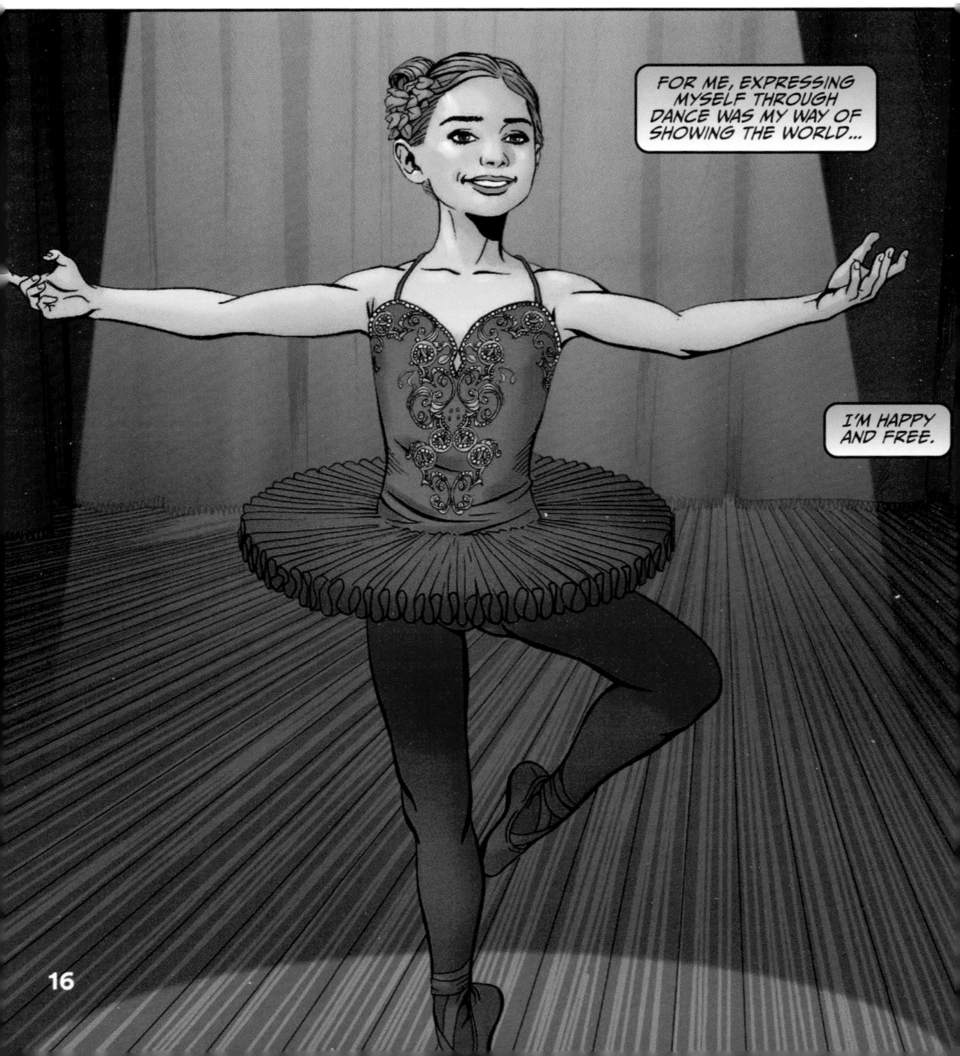
FOR ME, EXPRESSING MYSELF THROUGH DANCE WAS MY WAY OF SHOWING THE WORLD...
I'M HAPPY AND FREE.

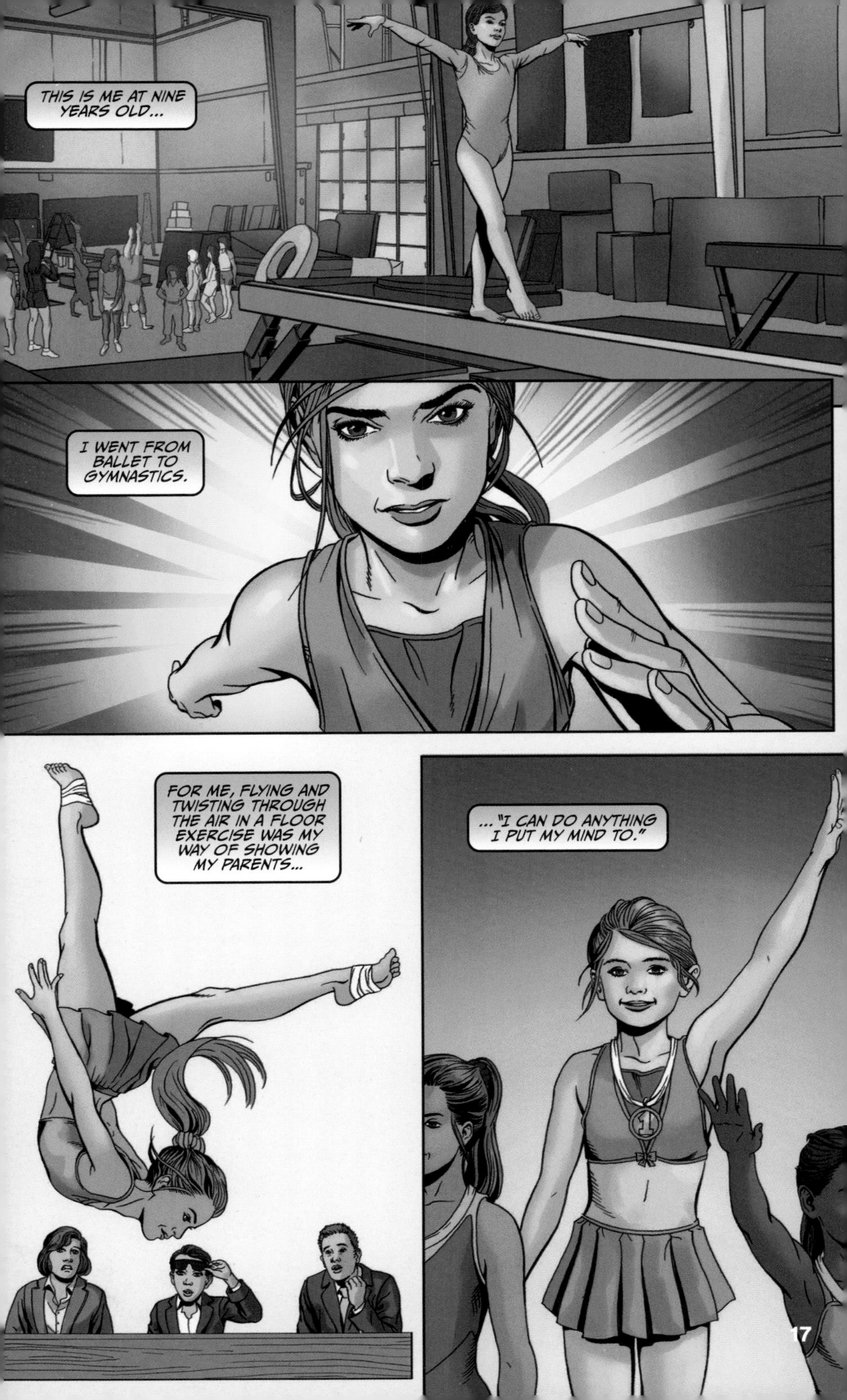
THIS IS ME AT NINE YEARS OLD...
I WENT FROM BALLET TO GYMNASTICS.
FOR ME, FLYING AND TWISTING THROUGH THE AIR IN A FLOOR EXERCISE WAS MY WAY OF SHOWING MY PARENTS...
..."I CAN DO ANYTHING I PUT MY MIND TO."

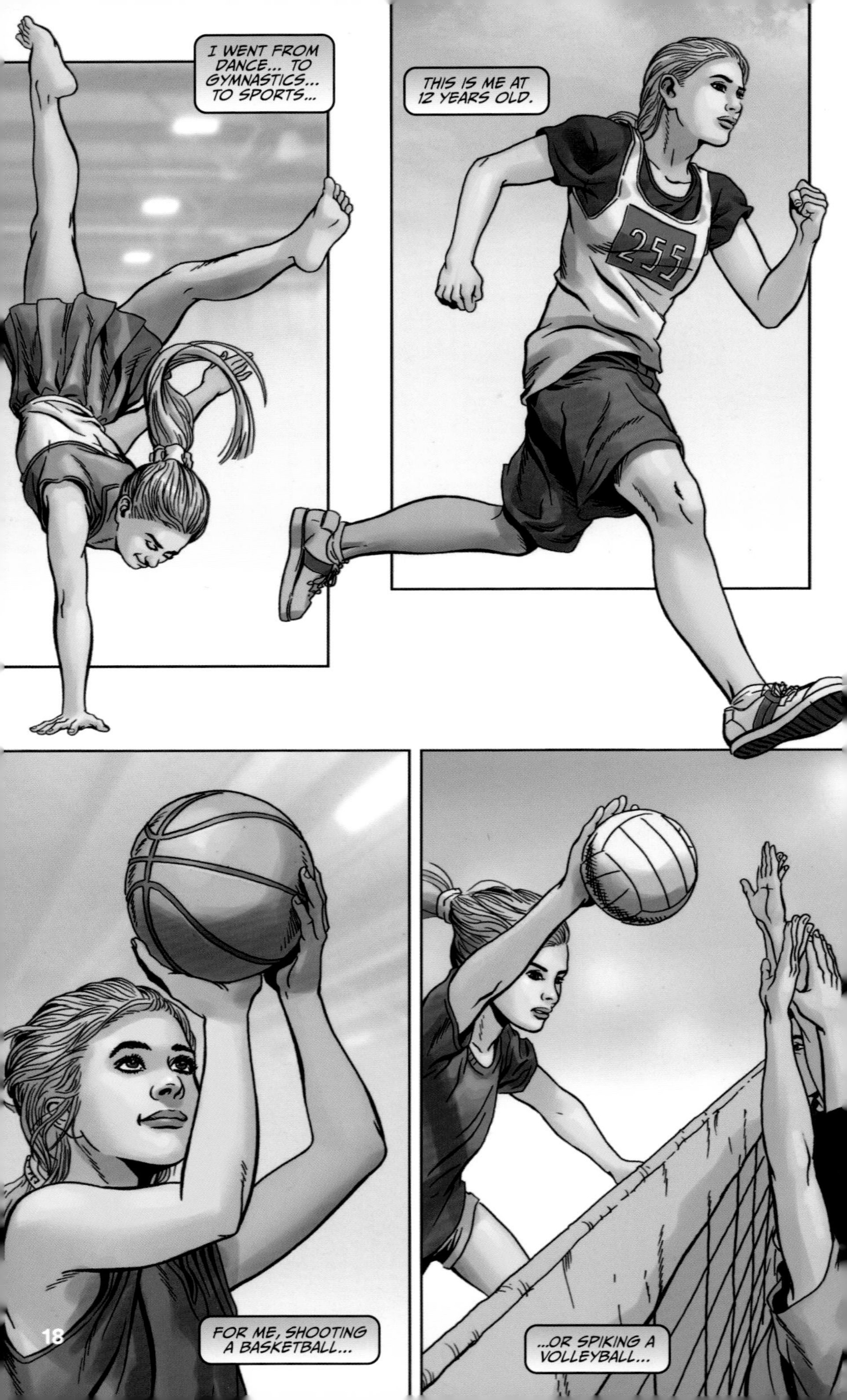
I WENT FROM DANCE... TO GYMNASTICS... TO SPORTS...
THIS IS ME AT 12 YEARS OLD.
255
FOR ME, SHOOTING A BASKETBALL...
...OR SPIKING A VOLLEYBALL...

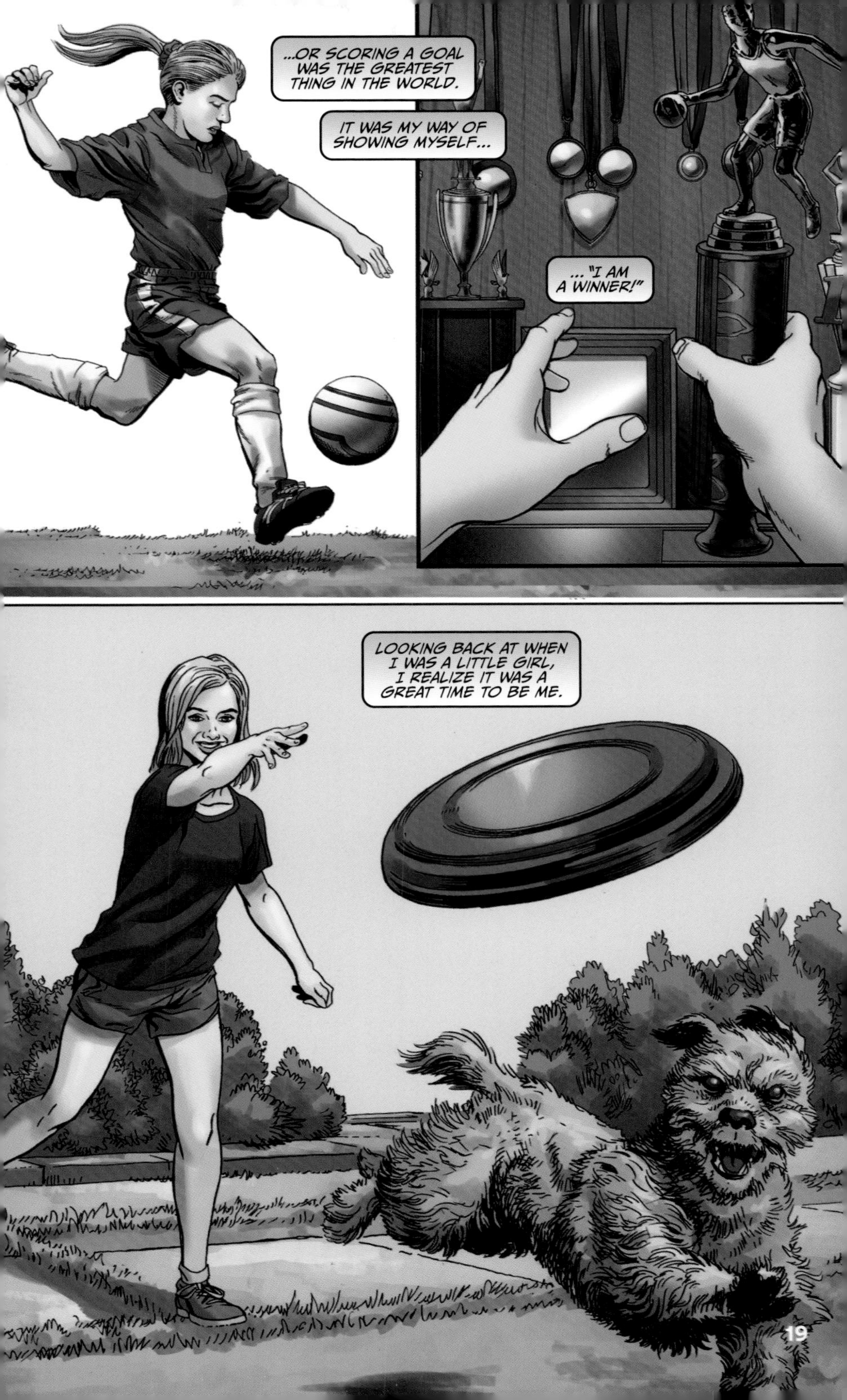
...OR SCORING A GOAL WAS THE GREATEST THING IN THE WORLD.
IT WAS MY WAY OF SHOWING MYSELF...
..."I AM A WINNER!"
LOOKING BACK AT WHEN I WAS A LITTLE GIRL, I REALIZE IT WAS A GREAT TIME TO BE ME.

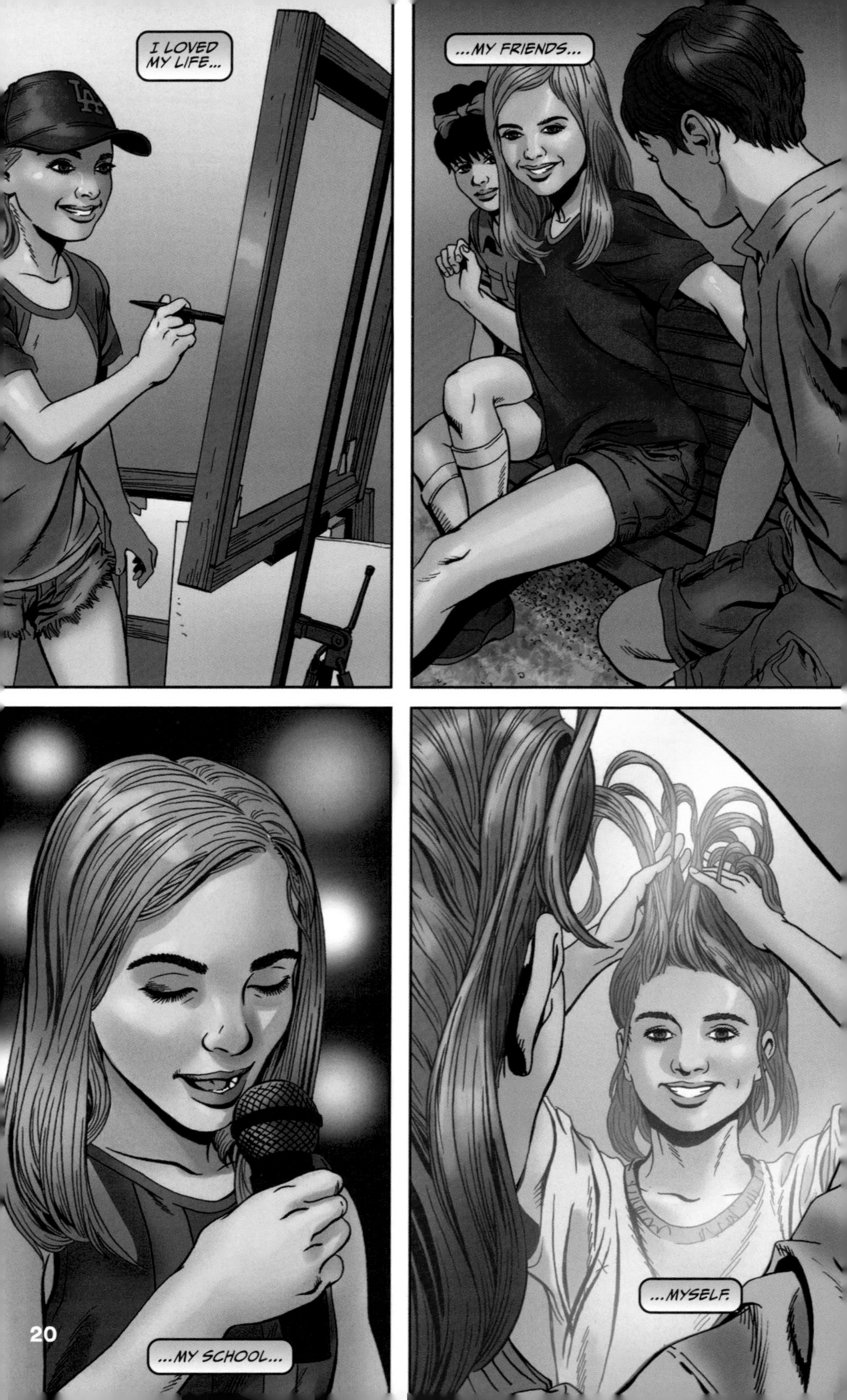
I LOVED MY LIFE...
...MY FRIENDS...
...MY SCHOOL...
...MYSELF.

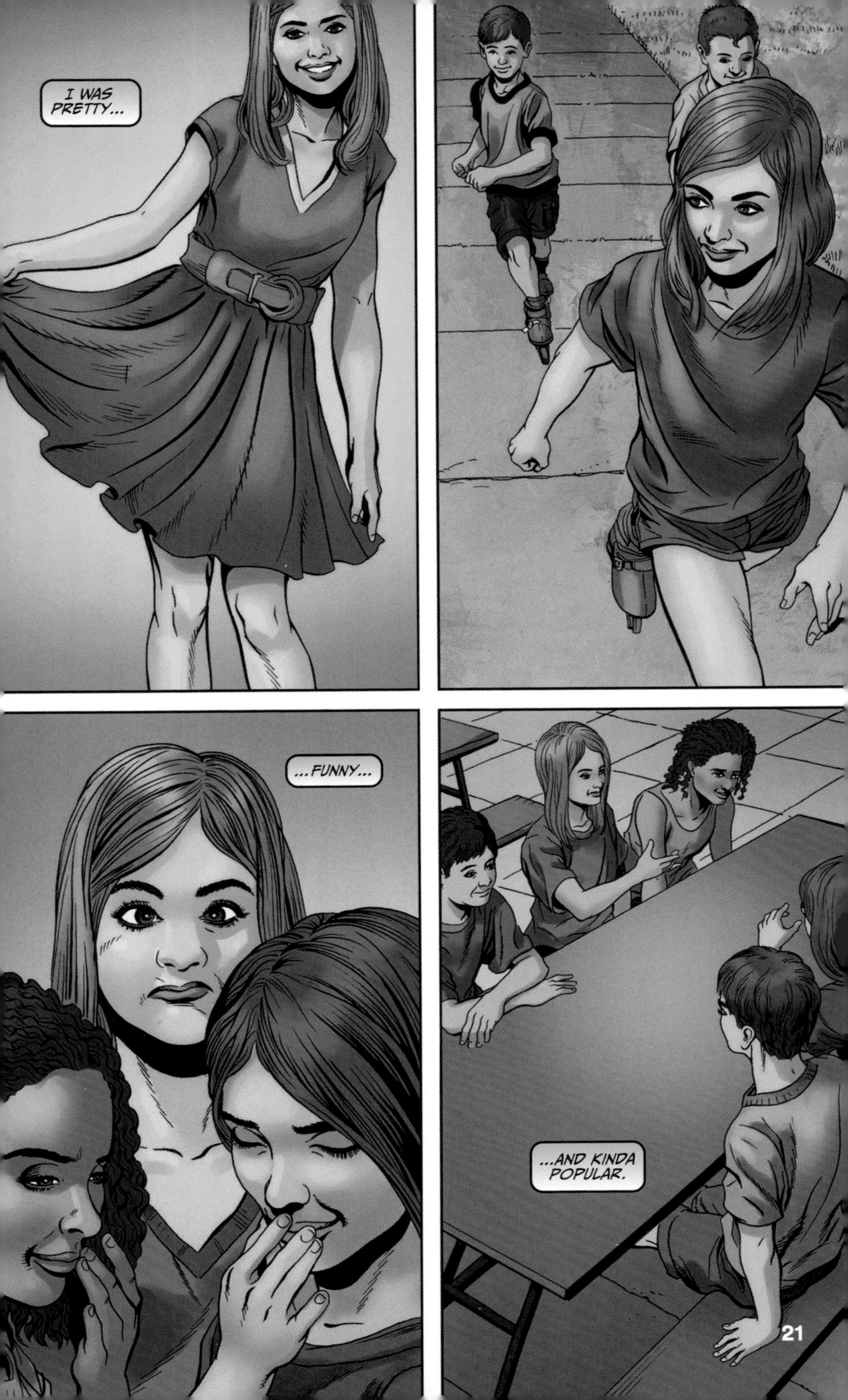
I WAS PRETTY...
...FUNNY...
...AND KINDA POPULAR.

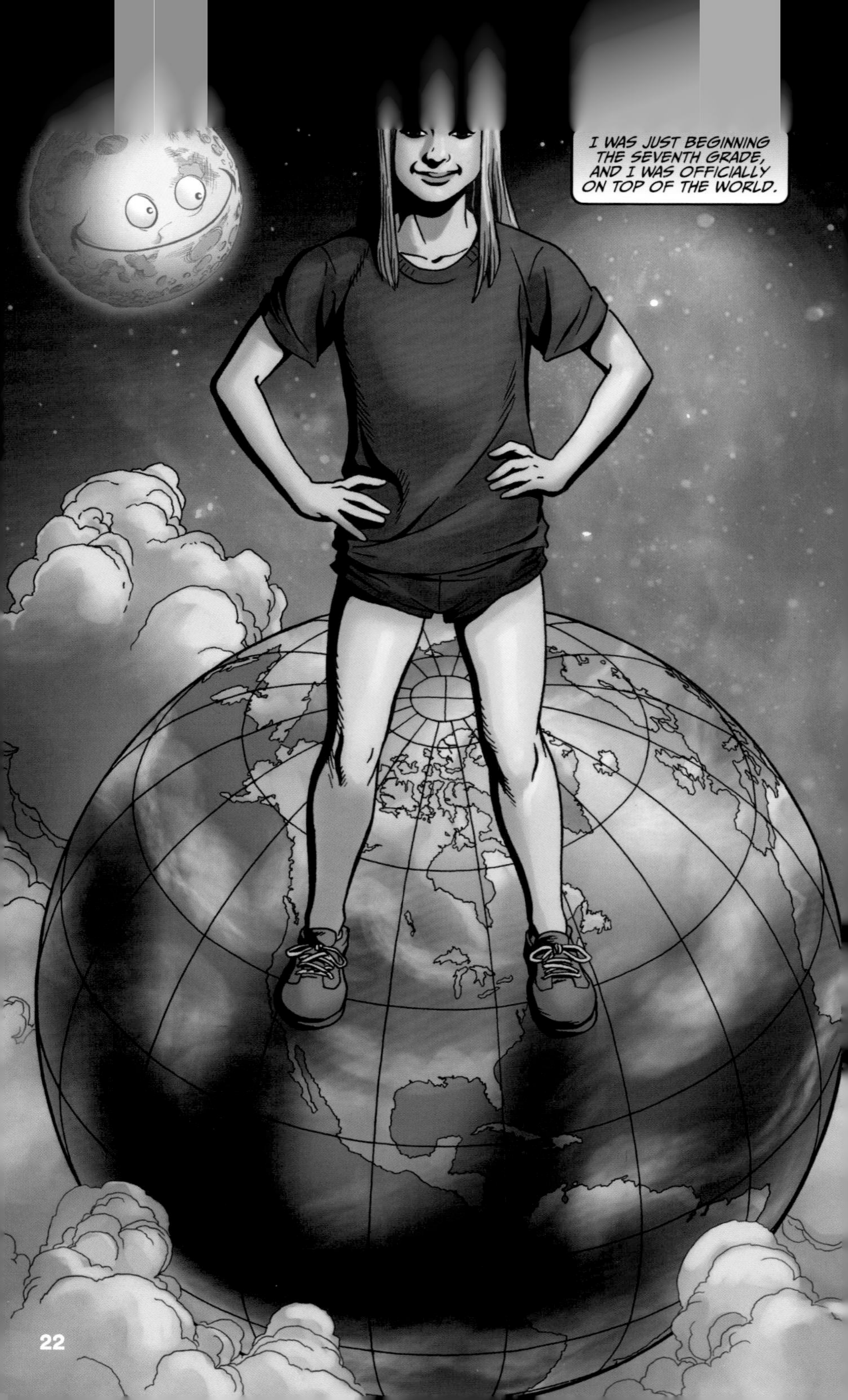
I WAS JUST BEGINNING THE SEVENTH GRADE, AND I WAS OFFICIALLY ON TOP OF THE WORLD.

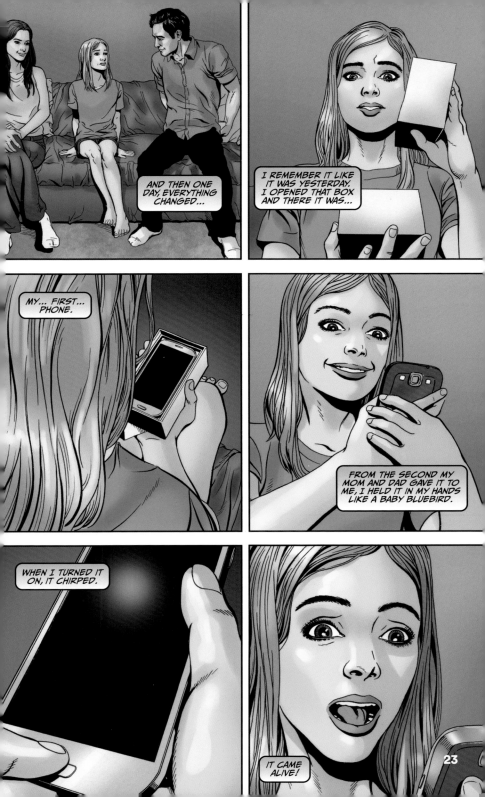

AND THEN ONE DAY, EVERYTHING CHANGED...

I REMEMBER IT LIKE IT WAS YESTERDAY. I OPENED THAT BOX AND THERE IT WAS...

MY... FIRST... PHONE.

FROM THE SECOND MY MOM AND DAD GAVE IT TO ME, I HELD IT IN MY HANDS LIKE A BABY BLUEBIRD.

WHEN I TURNED IT ON, IT CHIRPED.

IT CAME ALIVE!

23

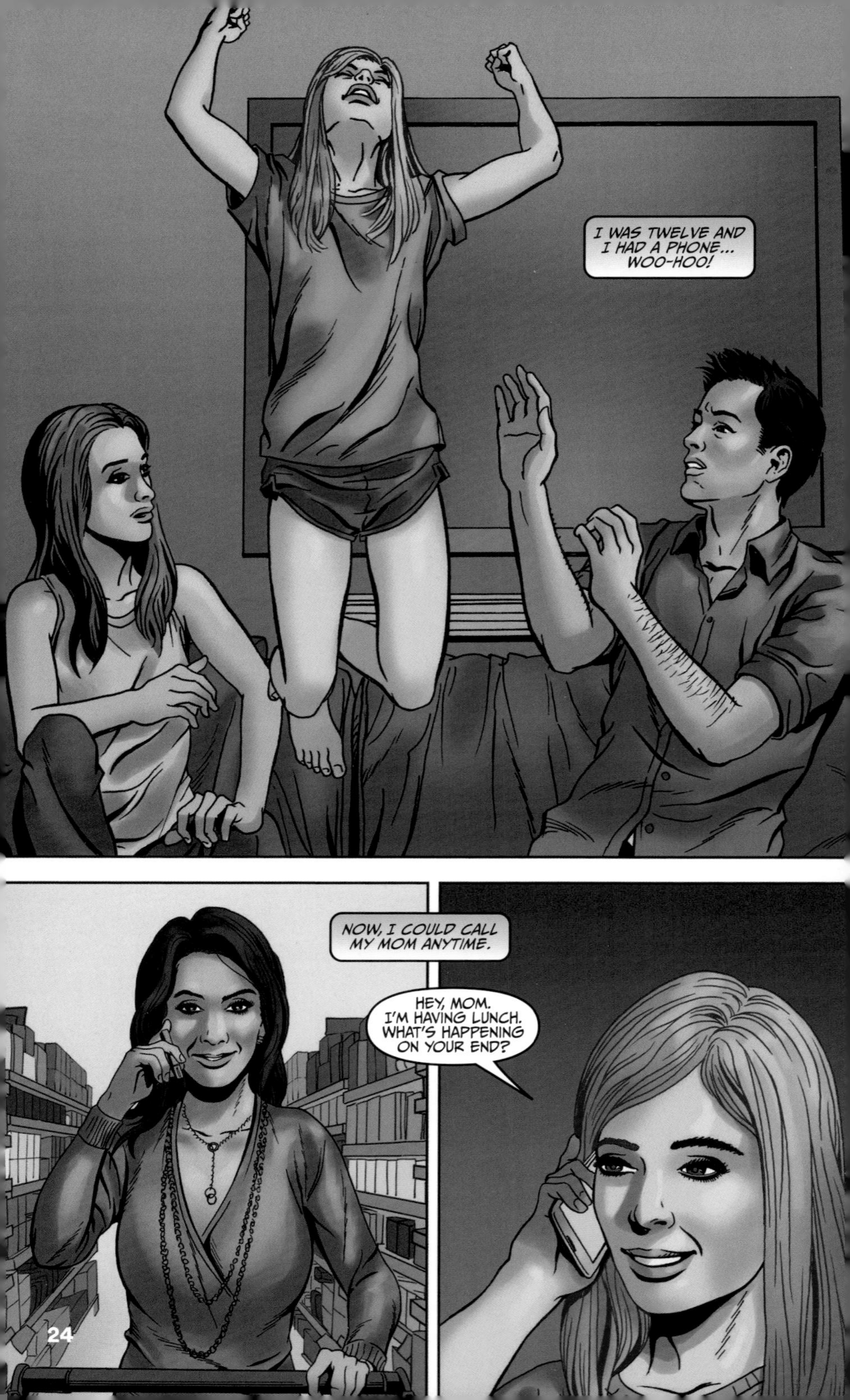
I WAS TWELVE AND I HAD A PHONE... WOO-HOO!
NOW, I COULD CALL MY MOM ANYTIME.
HEY, MOM. I'M HAVING LUNCH. WHAT'S HAPPENING ON YOUR END?

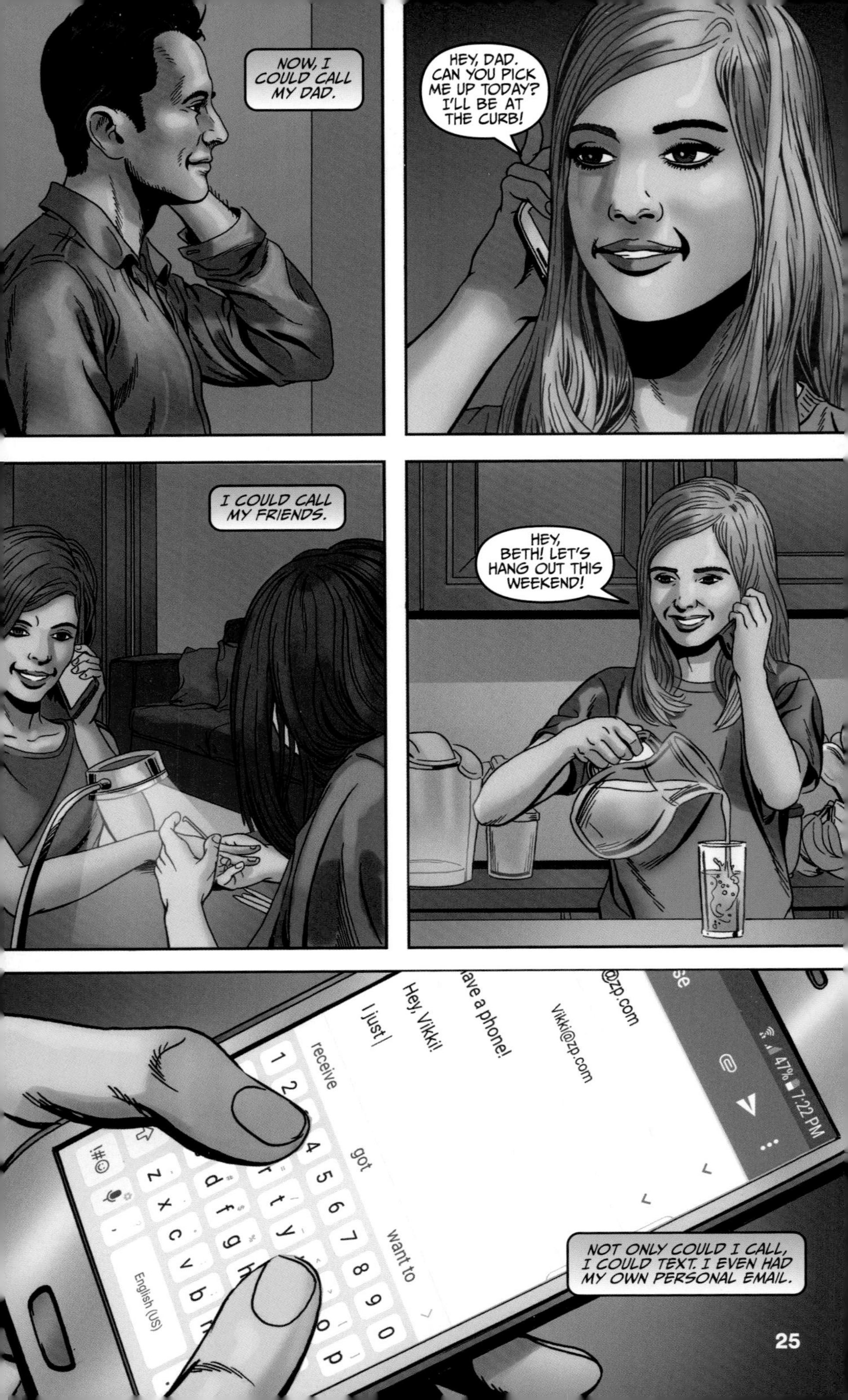
NOW, I COULD CALL MY DAD.
HEY, DAD. CAN YOU PICK ME UP TODAY? I'LL BE AT THE CURB!
I COULD CALL MY FRIENDS.
HEY, BETH! LET'S HANG OUT THIS WEEKEND!
Vikki@zp.com
Hey, Vikki!
I just
NOT ONLY COULD I CALL, I COULD TEXT. I EVEN HAD MY OWN PERSONAL EMAIL.

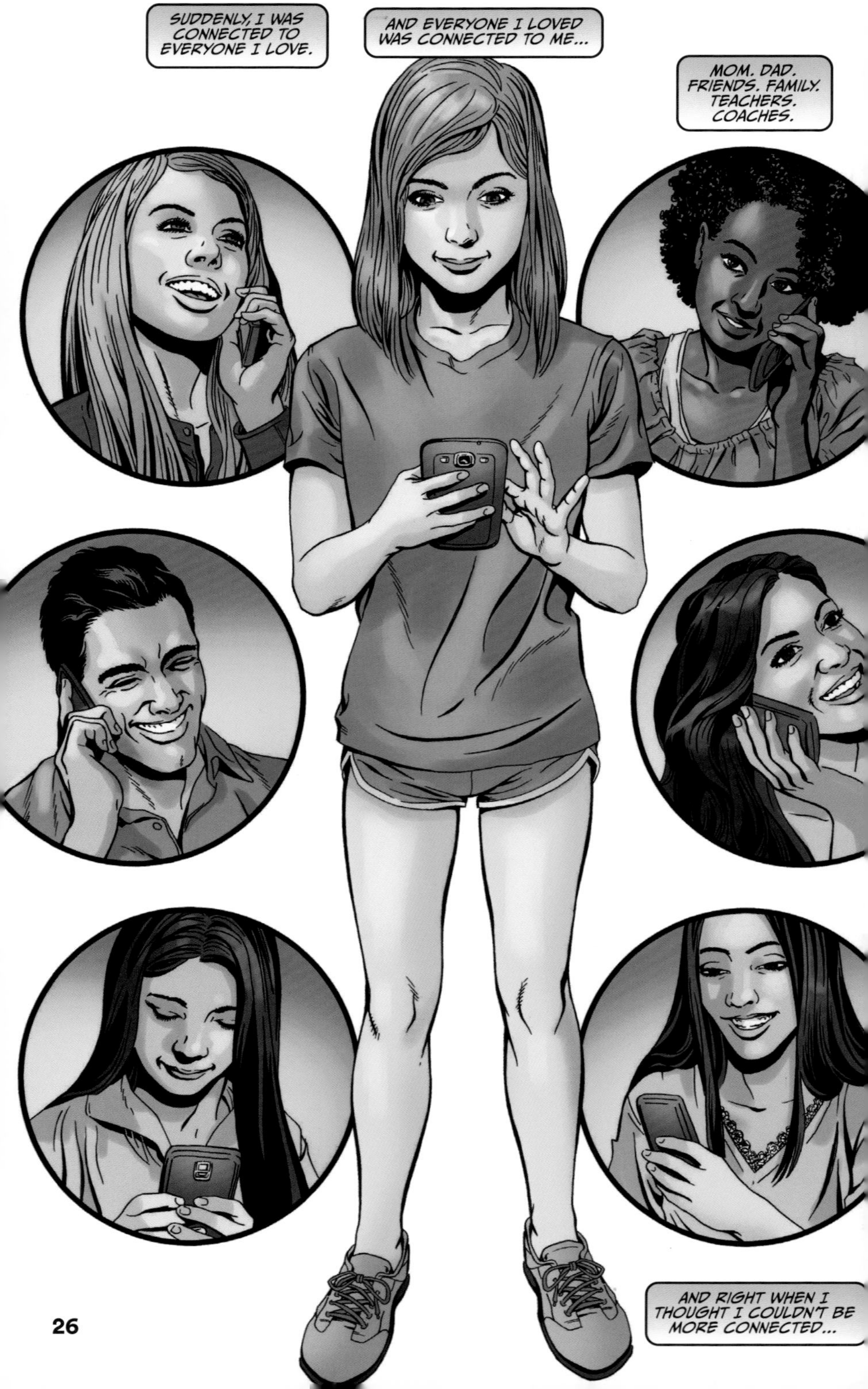
SUDDENLY, I WAS CONNECTED TO EVERYONE I LOVE.
AND EVERYONE I LOVED WAS CONNECTED TO ME...
MOM. DAD. FRIENDS. FAMILY. TEACHERS. COACHES.
AND RIGHT WHEN I THOUGHT I COULDN'T BE MORE CONNECTED...

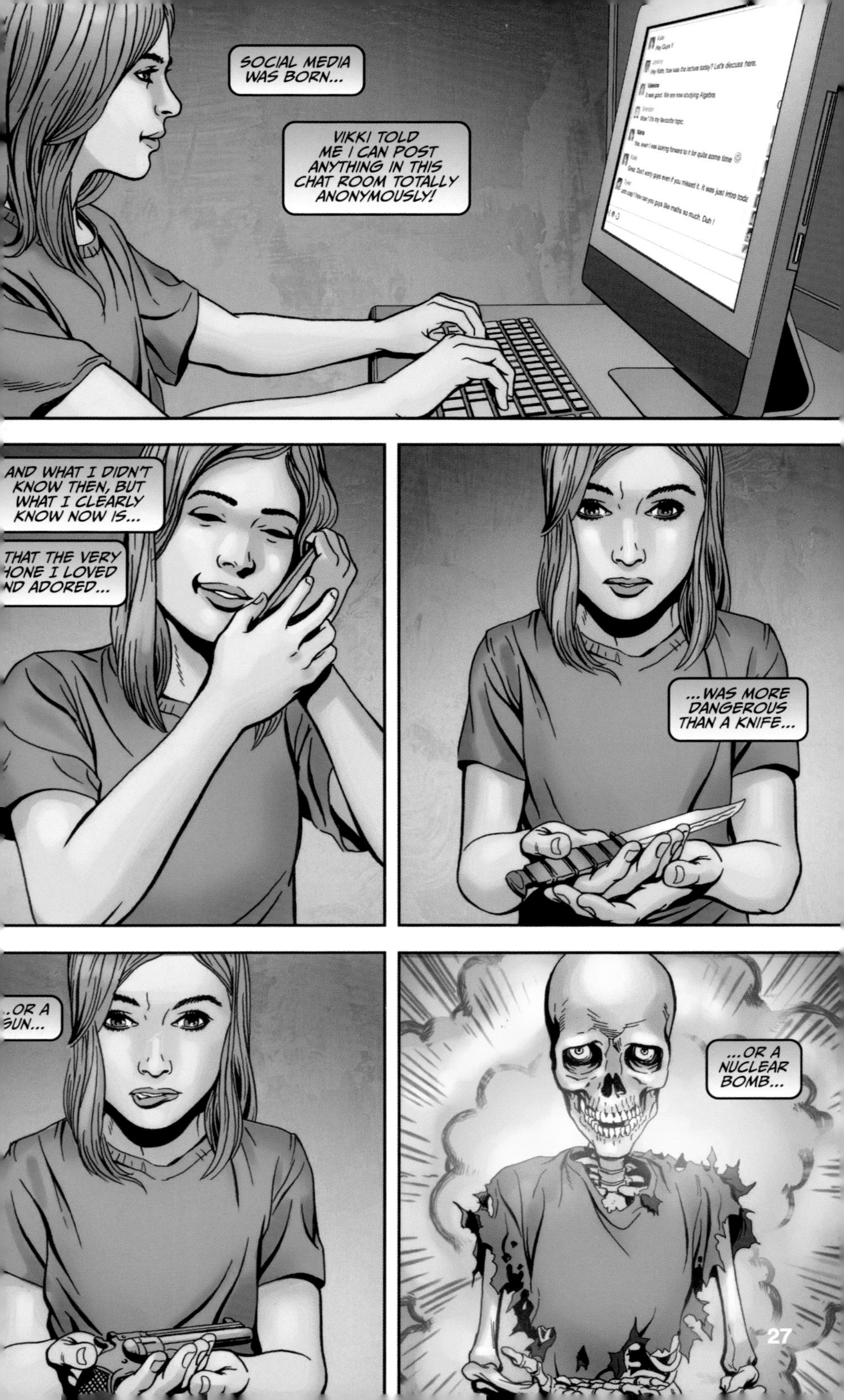
SOCIAL MEDIA WAS BORN...
VIKKI TOLD ME I CAN POST ANYTHING IN THIS CHAT ROOM TOTALLY ANONYMOUSLY!
Hey Kate, how was the lecture today? Let's discuss here.
It was good. We are now studying Algebra.
Wow! It's my favourite topic.
Yes, even I was looking forward to it for quite some time
AND WHAT I DIDN'T KNOW THEN, BUT WHAT I CLEARLY KNOW NOW IS...
THAT THE VERY HONE I LOVED ND ADORED...
...WAS MORE DANGEROUS THAN A KNIFE...
..OR A GUN...
...OR A NUCLEAR BOMB...

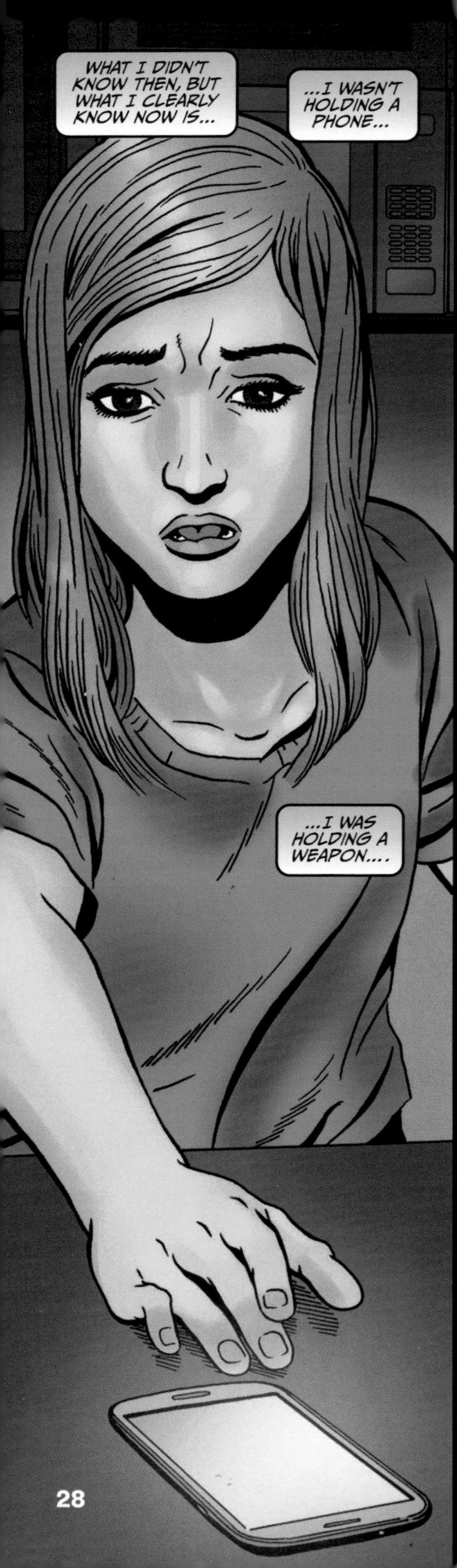
WHAT I DIDN'T KNOW THEN, BUT WHAT I CLEARLY KNOW NOW IS...
...I WASN'T HOLDING A PHONE...
...I WAS HOLDING A WEAPON....

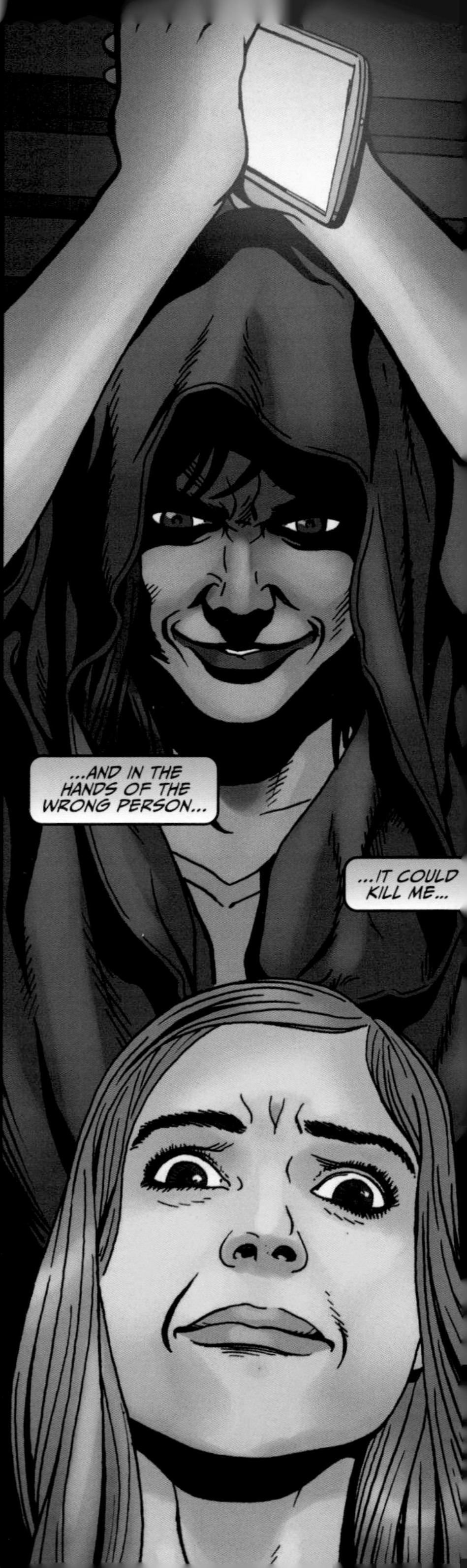
...AND IN THE HANDS OF THE WRONG PERSON...
...IT COULD KILL ME...

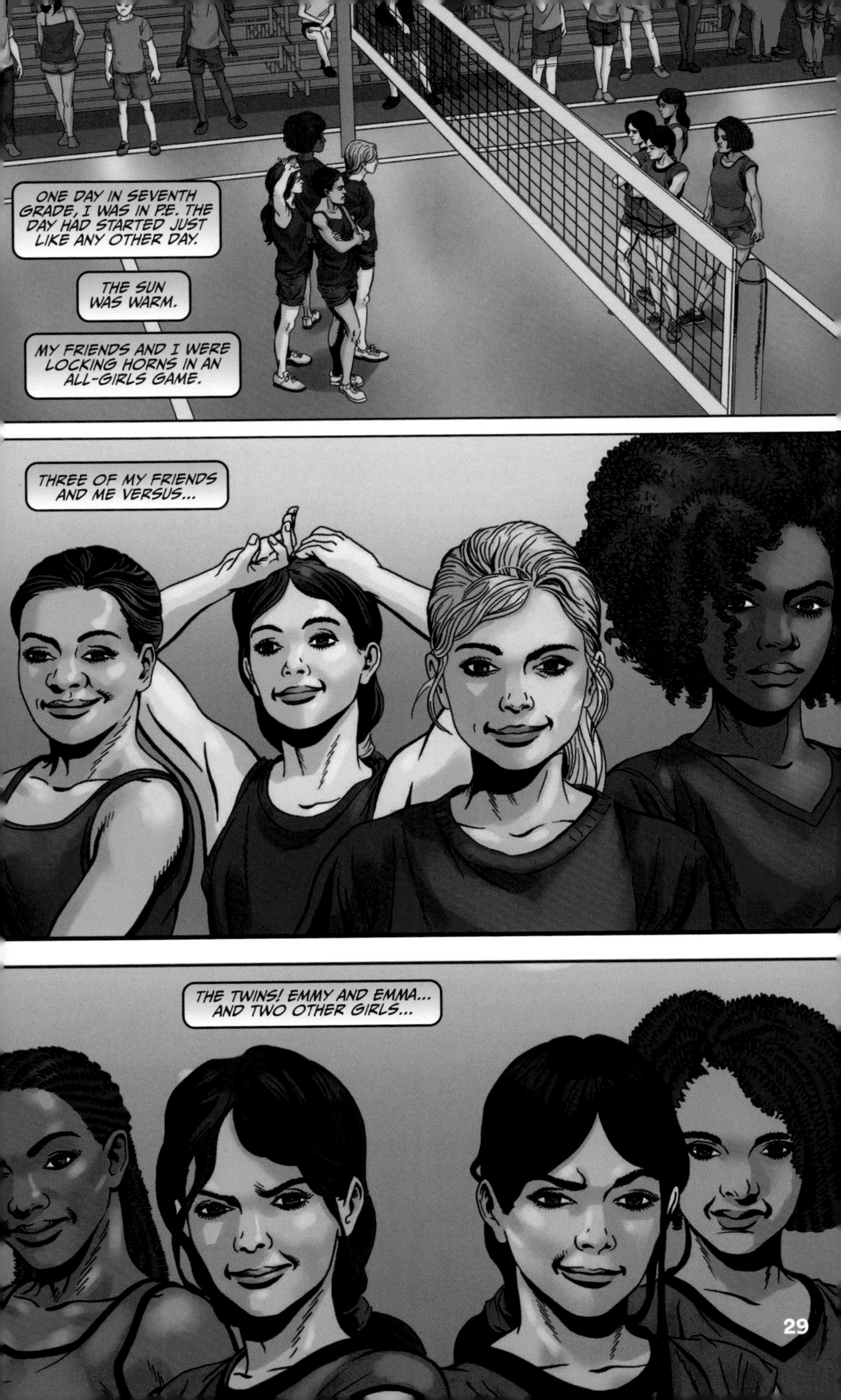
ONE DAY IN SEVENTH GRADE, I WAS IN P.E. THE DAY HAD STARTED JUST LIKE ANY OTHER DAY.
THE SUN WAS WARM.
MY FRIENDS AND I WERE LOCKING HORNS IN AN ALL-GIRLS GAME.
THREE OF MY FRIENDS AND ME VERSUS...
THE TWINS! EMMY AND EMMA... AND TWO OTHER GIRLS...

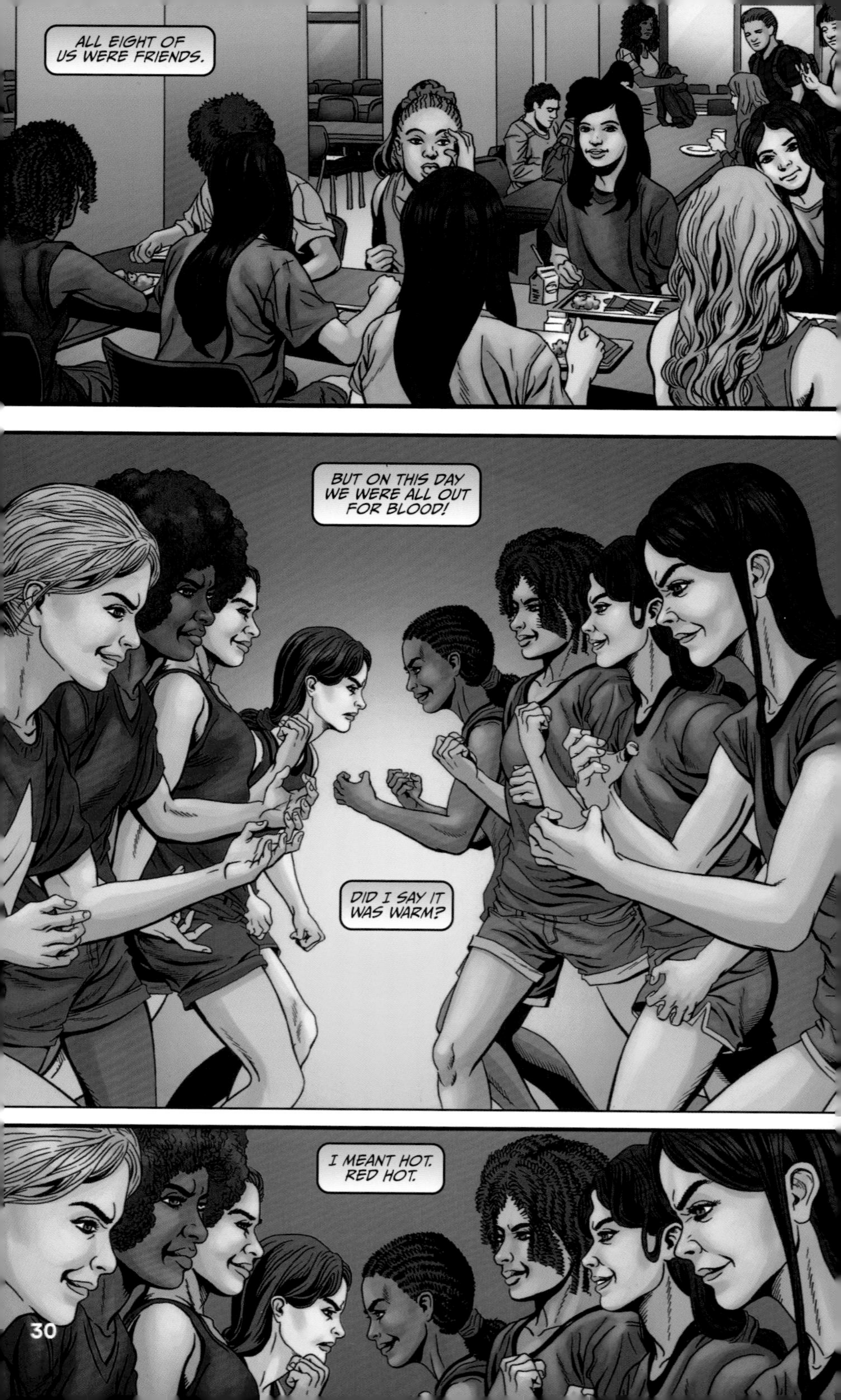
ALL EIGHT OF US WERE FRIENDS.
BUT ON THIS DAY WE WERE ALL OUT FOR BLOOD!
DID I SAY IT WAS WARM?
I MEANT HOT. RED HOT.

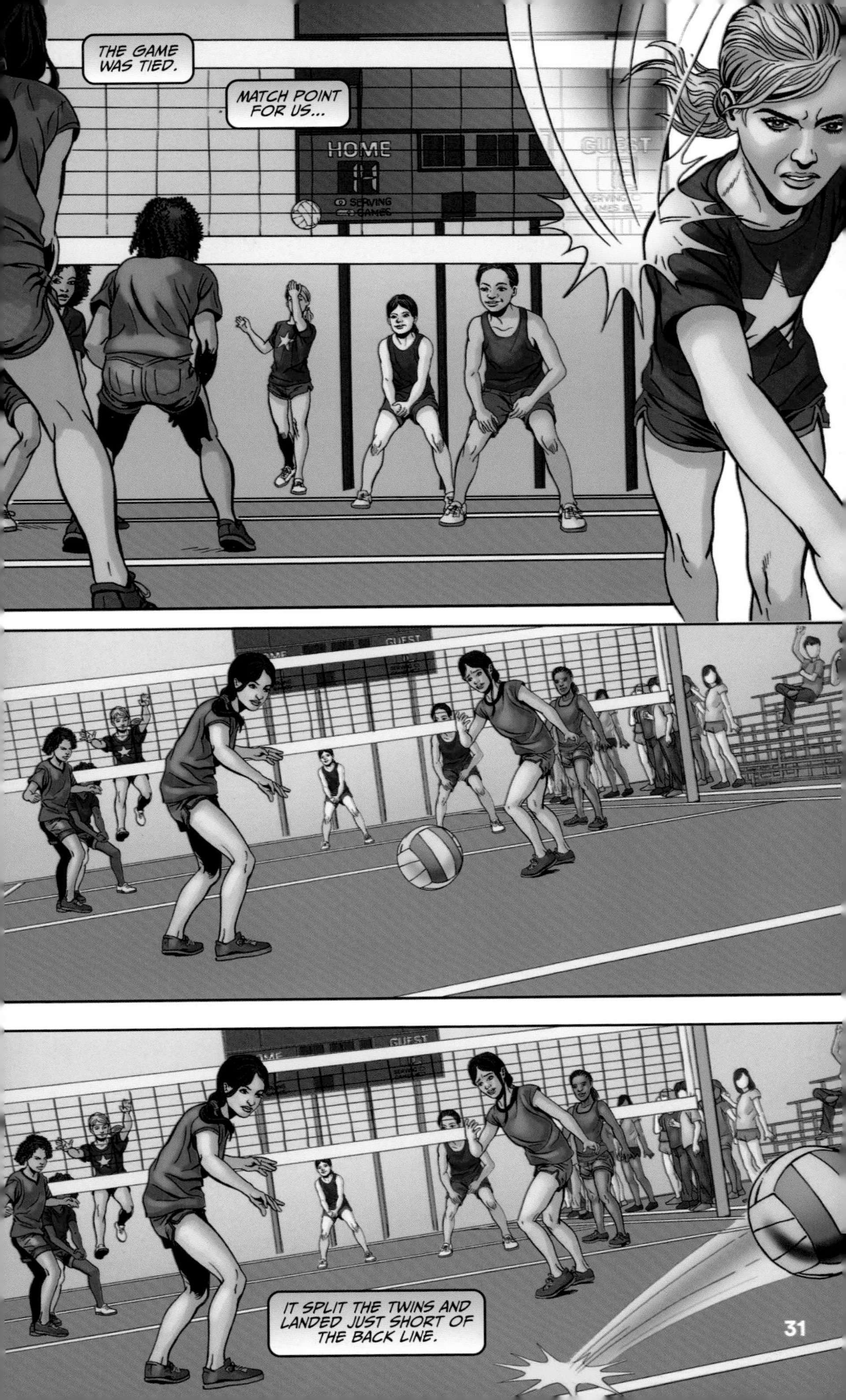
THE GAME WAS TIED.
MATCH POINT FOR US...
HOME
GUEST
SERVING
GAMES
IT SPLIT THE TWINS AND LANDED JUST SHORT OF THE BACK LINE.

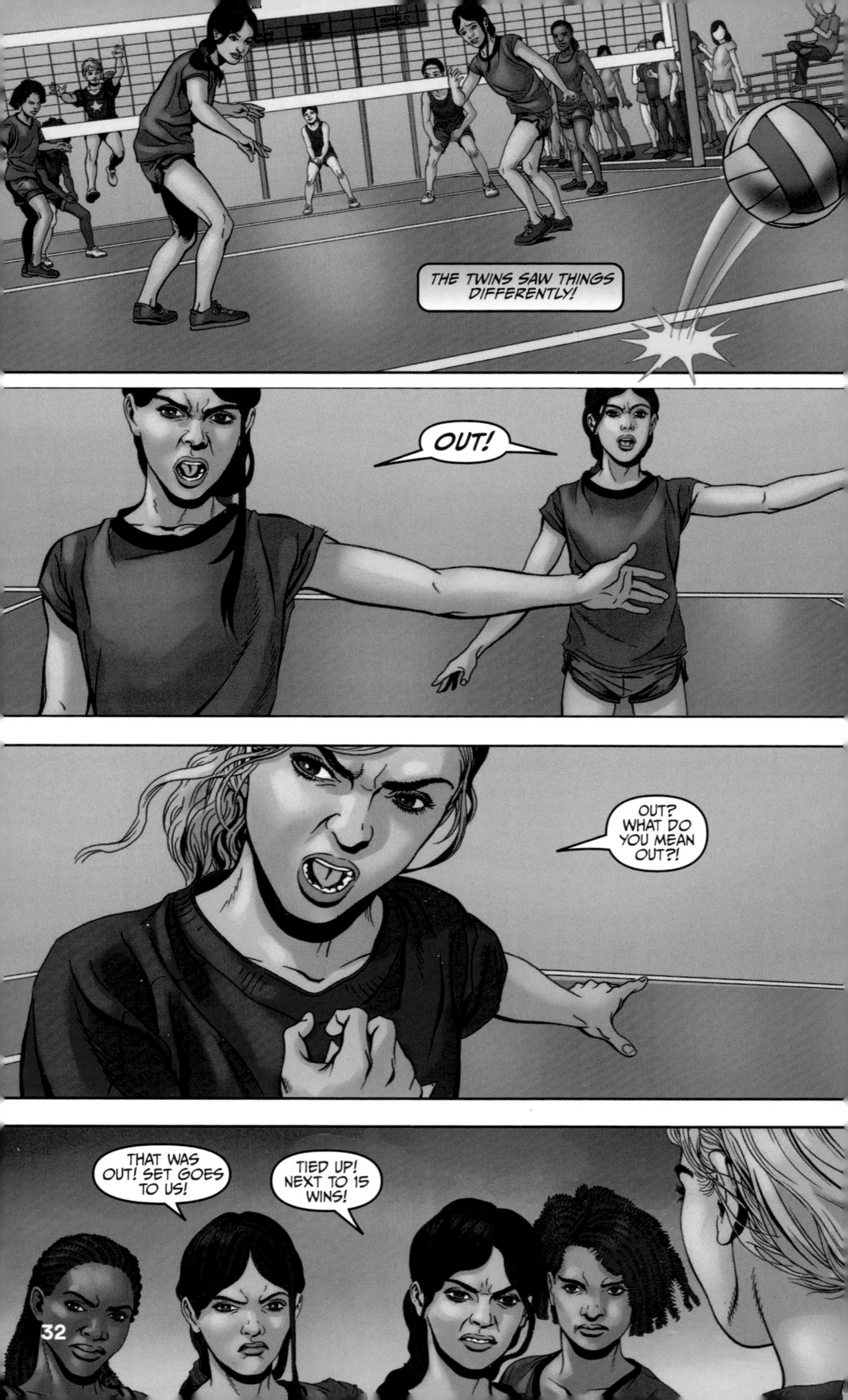
THE TWINS SAW THINGS DIFFERENTLY!
OUT!
OUT? WHAT DO YOU MEAN OUT?!
THAT WAS OUT! SET GOES TO US!
TIED UP! NEXT TO 15 WINS!

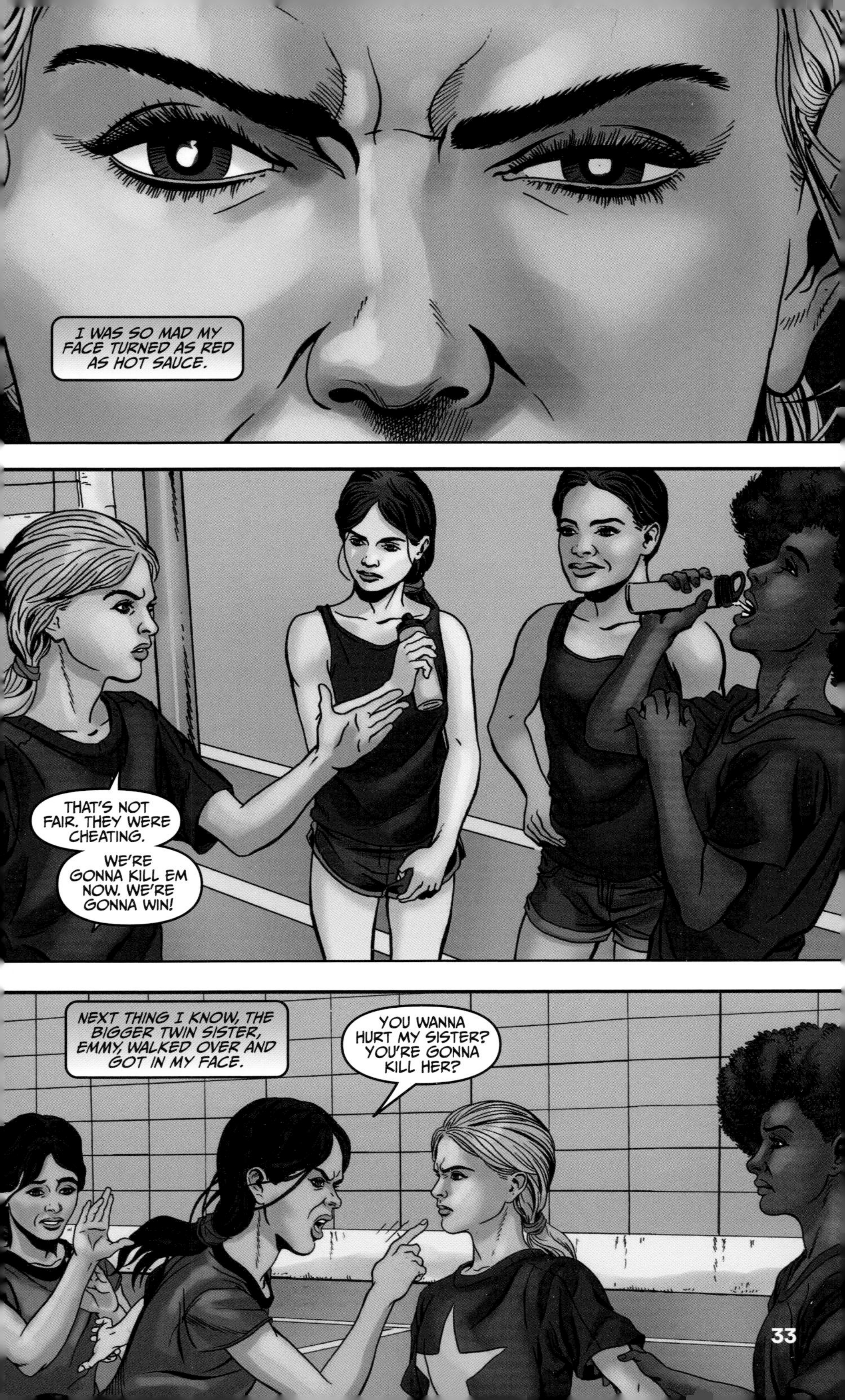
I WAS SO MAD MY FACE TURNED AS RED AS HOT SAUCE.
THAT'S NOT FAIR. THEY WERE CHEATING.
WE'RE GONNA KILL EM NOW. WE'RE GONNA WIN!
NEXT THING I KNOW, THE BIGGER TWIN SISTER, EMMY, WALKED OVER AND GOT IN MY FACE.
YOU WANNA HURT MY SISTER? YOU'RE GONNA KILL HER?

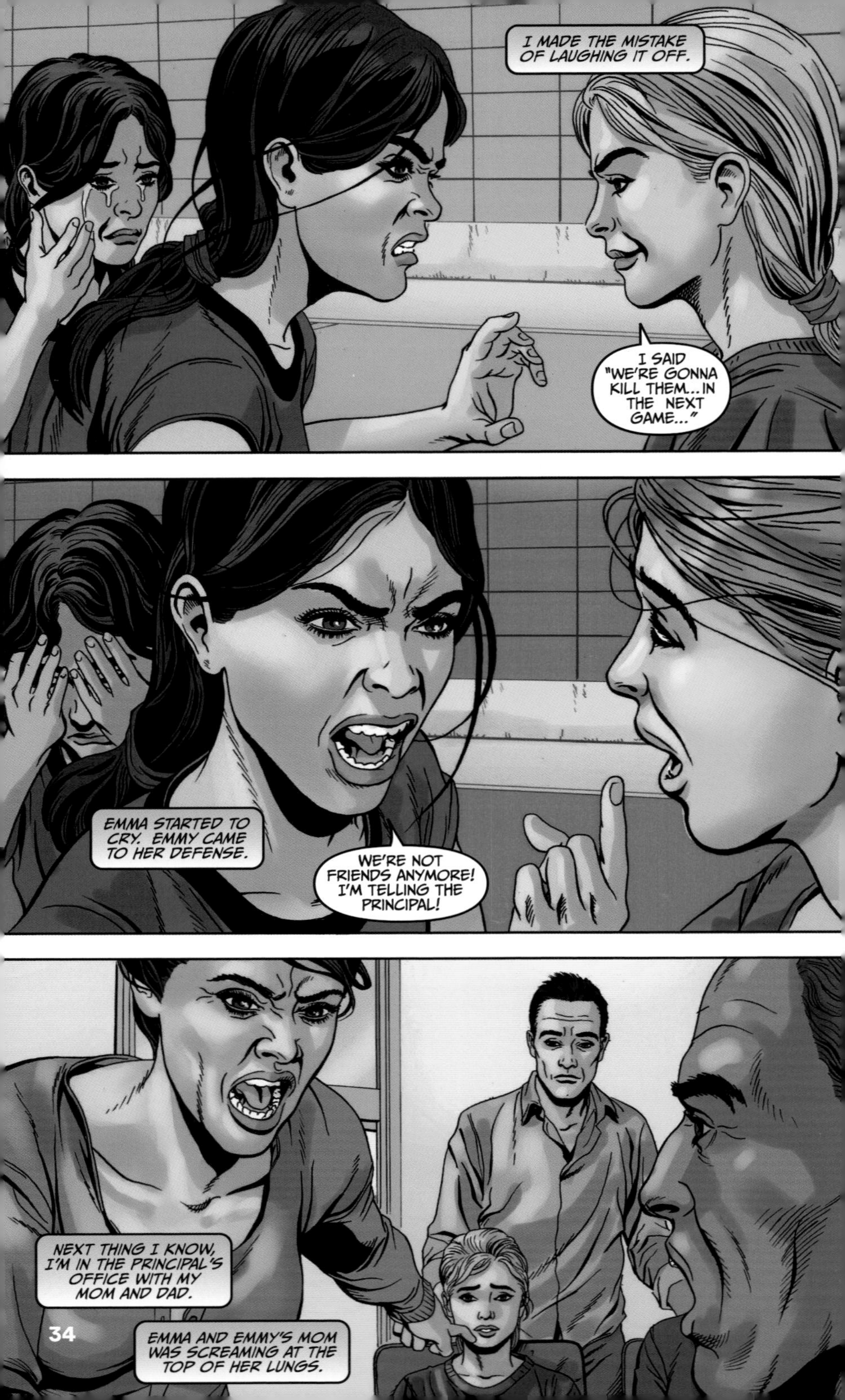
I MADE THE MISTAKE OF LAUGHING IT OFF.
I SAID "WE'RE GONNA KILL THEM...IN THE NEXT GAME..."
EMMA STARTED TO CRY. EMMY CAME TO HER DEFENSE.
WE'RE NOT FRIENDS ANYMORE! I'M TELLING THE PRINCIPAL!
NEXT THING I KNOW, I'M IN THE PRINCIPAL'S OFFICE WITH MY MOM AND DAD.
EMMA AND EMMY'S MOM WAS SCREAMING AT THE TOP OF HER LUNGS.

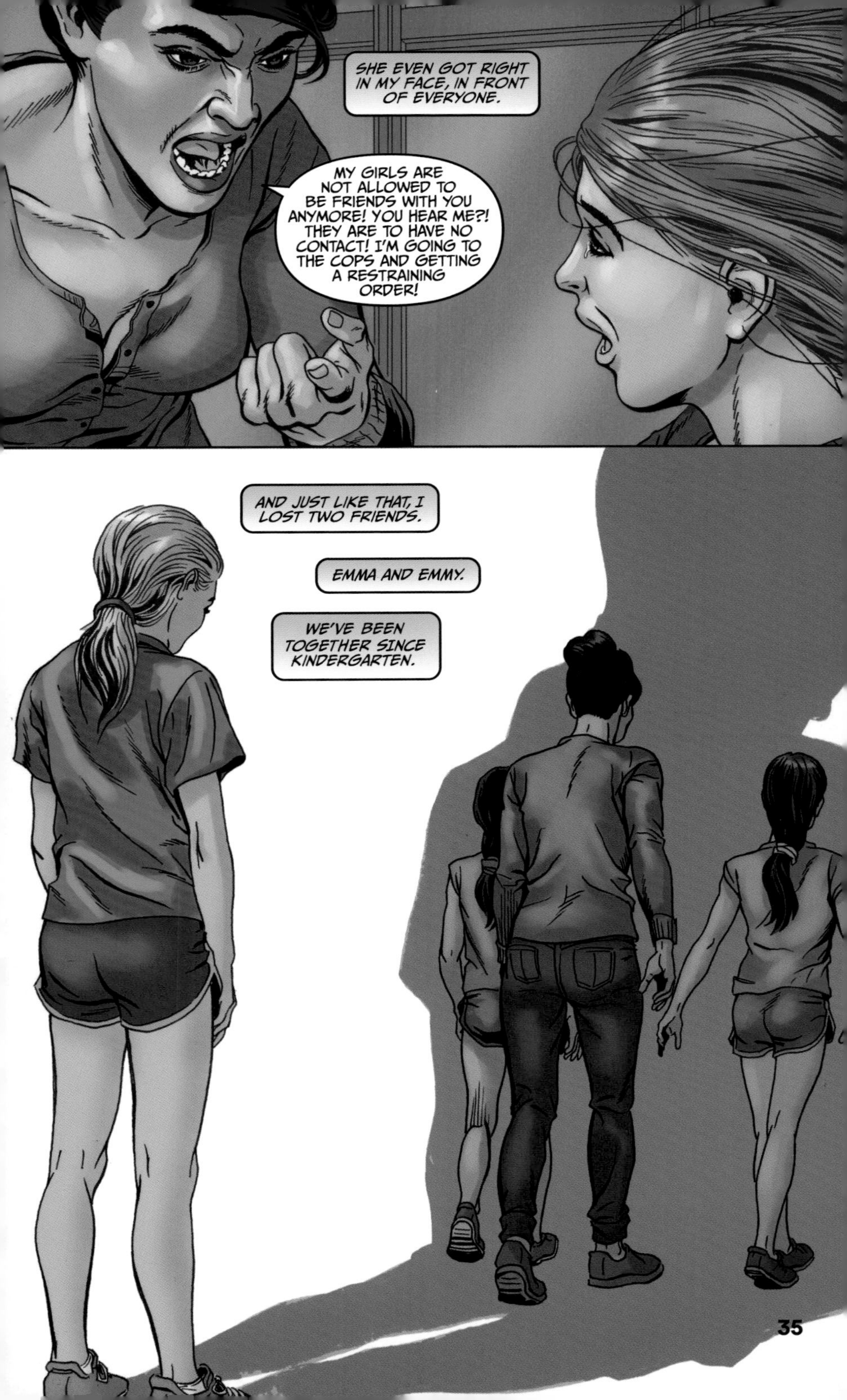
SHE EVEN GOT RIGHT IN MY FACE, IN FRONT OF EVERYONE.
MY GIRLS ARE NOT ALLOWED TO BE FRIENDS WITH YOU ANYMORE! YOU HEAR ME?! THEY ARE TO HAVE NO CONTACT! I'M GOING TO THE COPS AND GETTING A RESTRAINING ORDER!
AND JUST LIKE THAT, I LOST TWO FRIENDS.
EMMA AND EMMY.
WE'VE BEEN TOGETHER SINCE KINDERGARTEN.

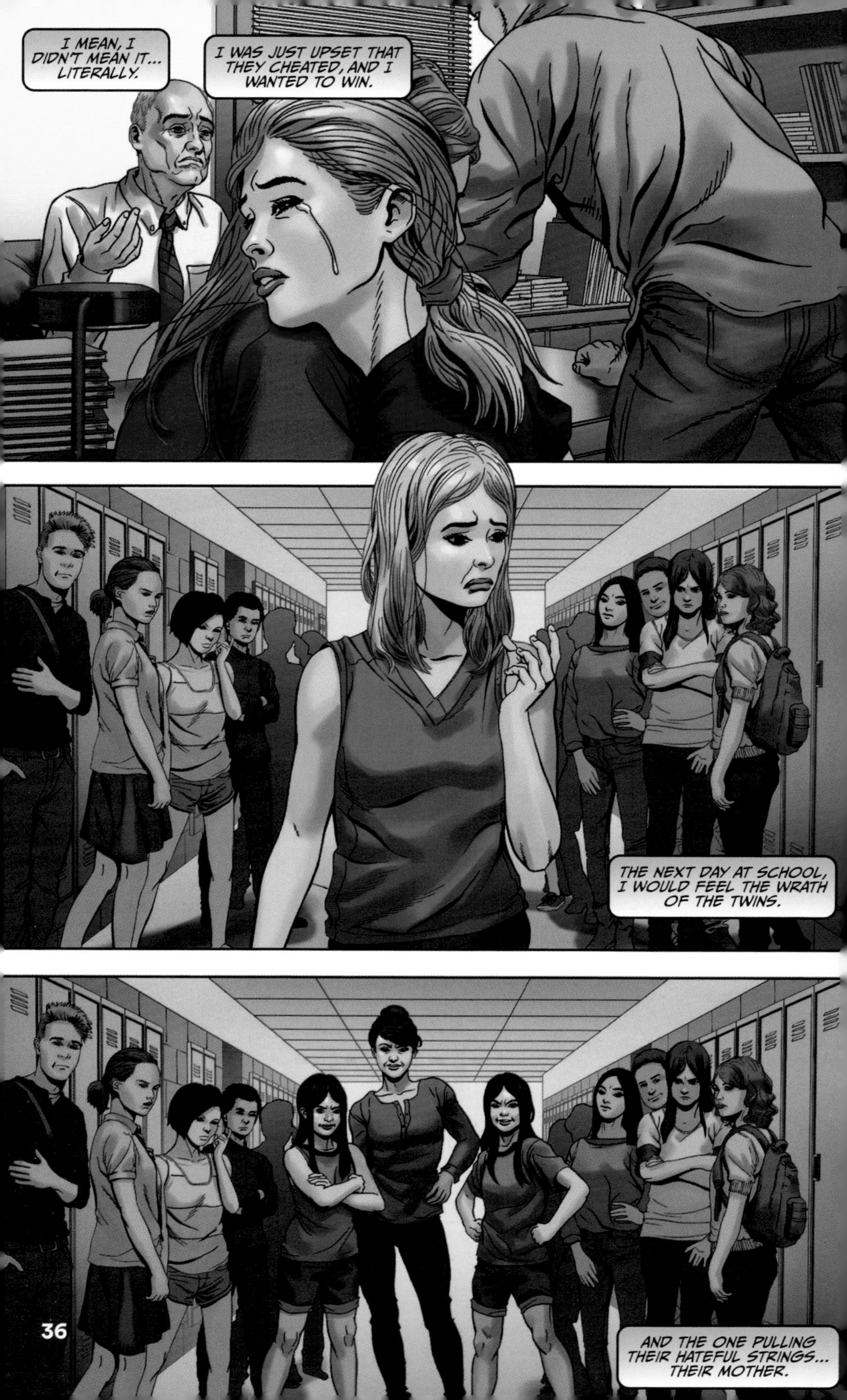
I MEAN, I DIDN'T MEAN IT... LITERALLY.
I WAS JUST UPSET THAT THEY CHEATED, AND I WANTED TO WIN.
THE NEXT DAY AT SCHOOL, I WOULD FEEL THE WRATH OF THE TWINS.
AND THE ONE PULLING THEIR HATEFUL STRINGS... THEIR MOTHER.

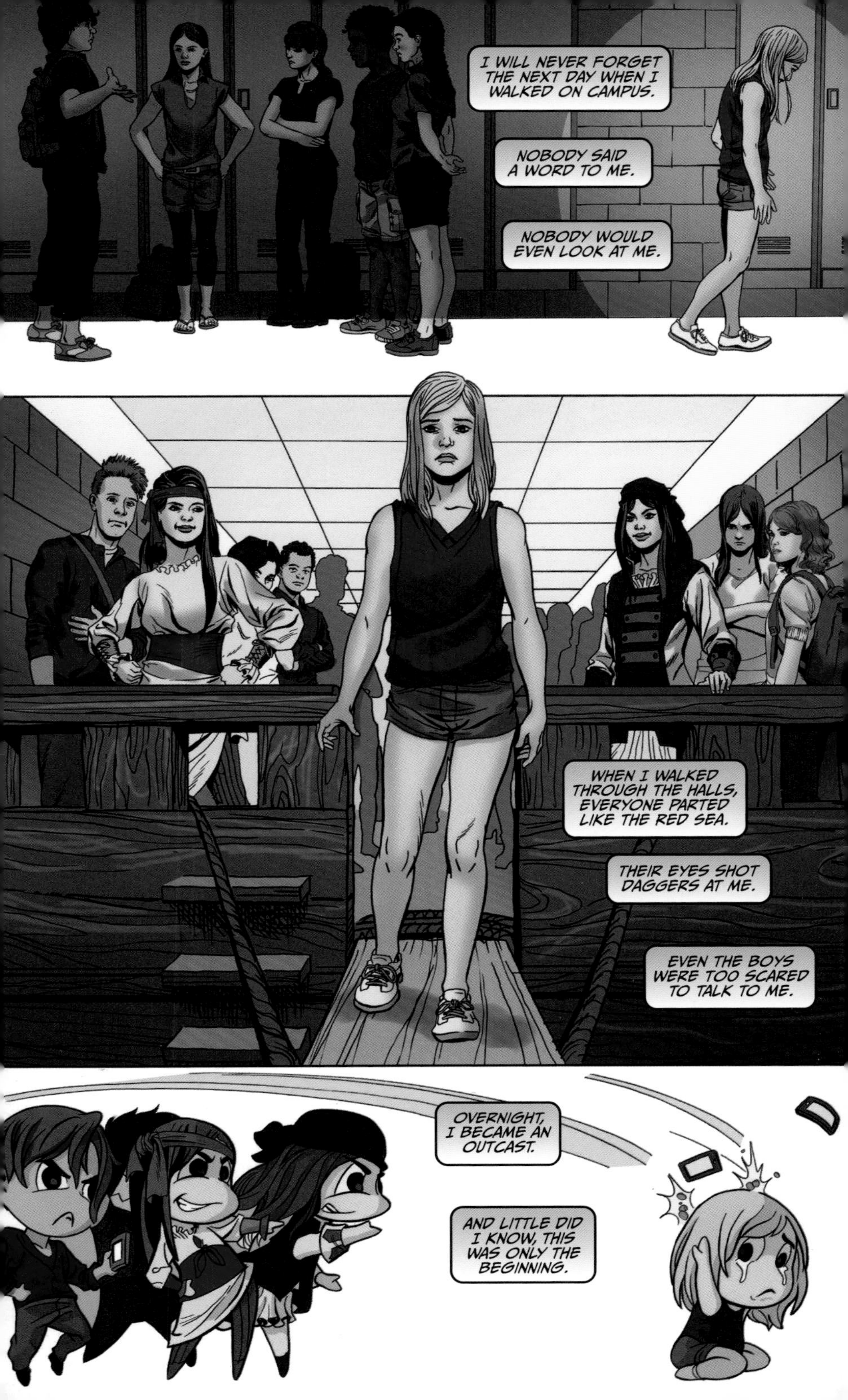
I WILL NEVER FORGET THE NEXT DAY WHEN I WALKED ON CAMPUS.
NOBODY SAID A WORD TO ME.
NOBODY WOULD EVEN LOOK AT ME.
WHEN I WALKED THROUGH THE HALLS, EVERYONE PARTED LIKE THE RED SEA.
THEIR EYES SHOT DAGGERS AT ME.
EVEN THE BOYS WERE TOO SCARED TO TALK TO ME.
OVERNIGHT, I BECAME AN OUTCAST.
AND LITTLE DID I KNOW, THIS WAS ONLY THE BEGINNING.

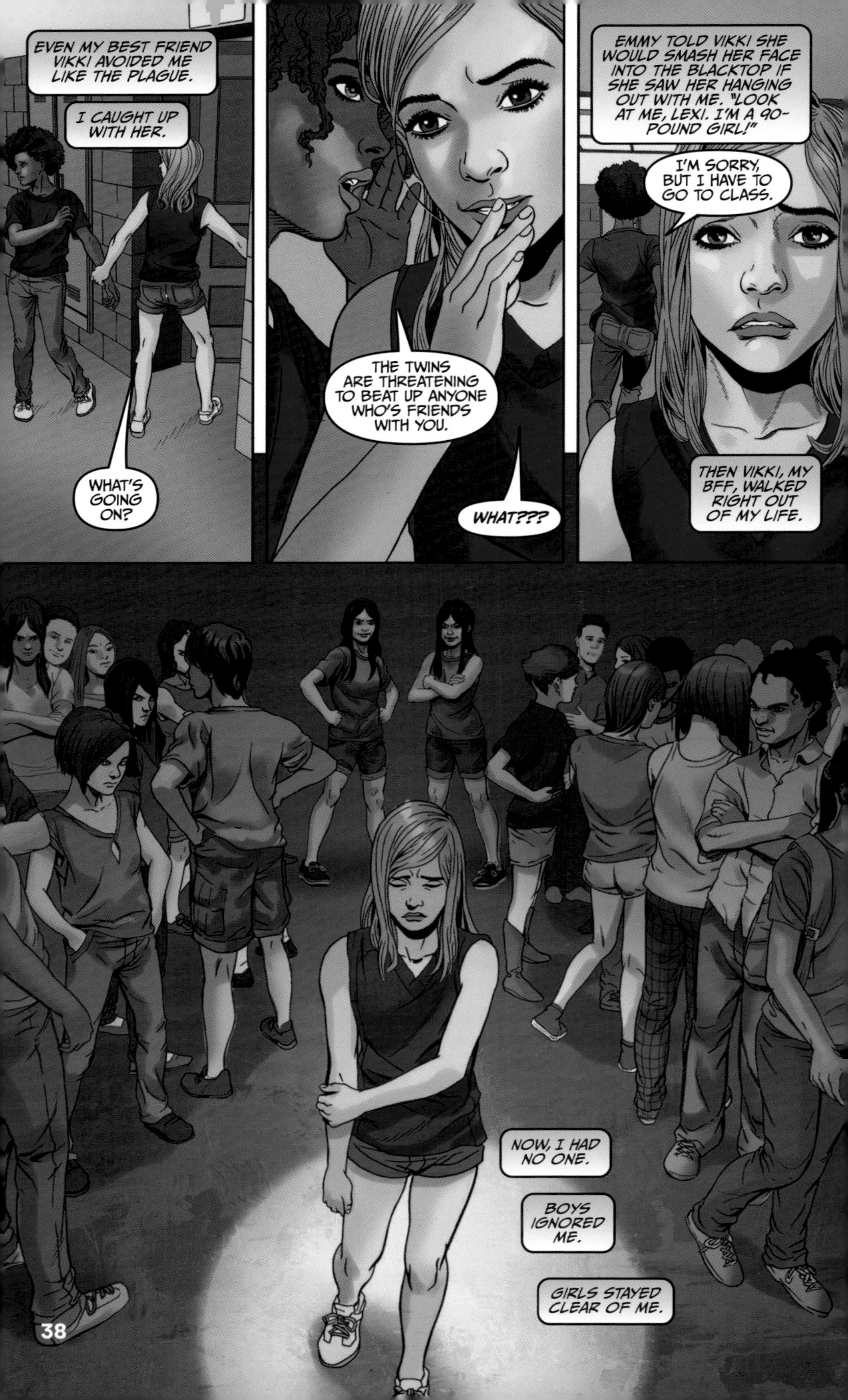

EVEN MY BEST FRIEND VIKKI AVOIDED ME LIKE THE PLAGUE.
I CAUGHT UP WITH HER.
WHAT'S GOING ON?
THE TWINS ARE THREATENING TO BEAT UP ANYONE WHO'S FRIENDS WITH YOU.
WHAT???
EMMY TOLD VIKKI SHE WOULD SMASH HER FACE INTO THE BLACKTOP IF SHE SAW HER HANGING OUT WITH ME. "LOOK AT ME, LEXI. I'M A 90-POUND GIRL!"
I'M SORRY, BUT I HAVE TO GO TO CLASS.
THEN VIKKI, MY BFF, WALKED RIGHT OUT OF MY LIFE.
NOW, I HAD NO ONE.
BOYS IGNORED ME.
GIRLS STAYED CLEAR OF ME.

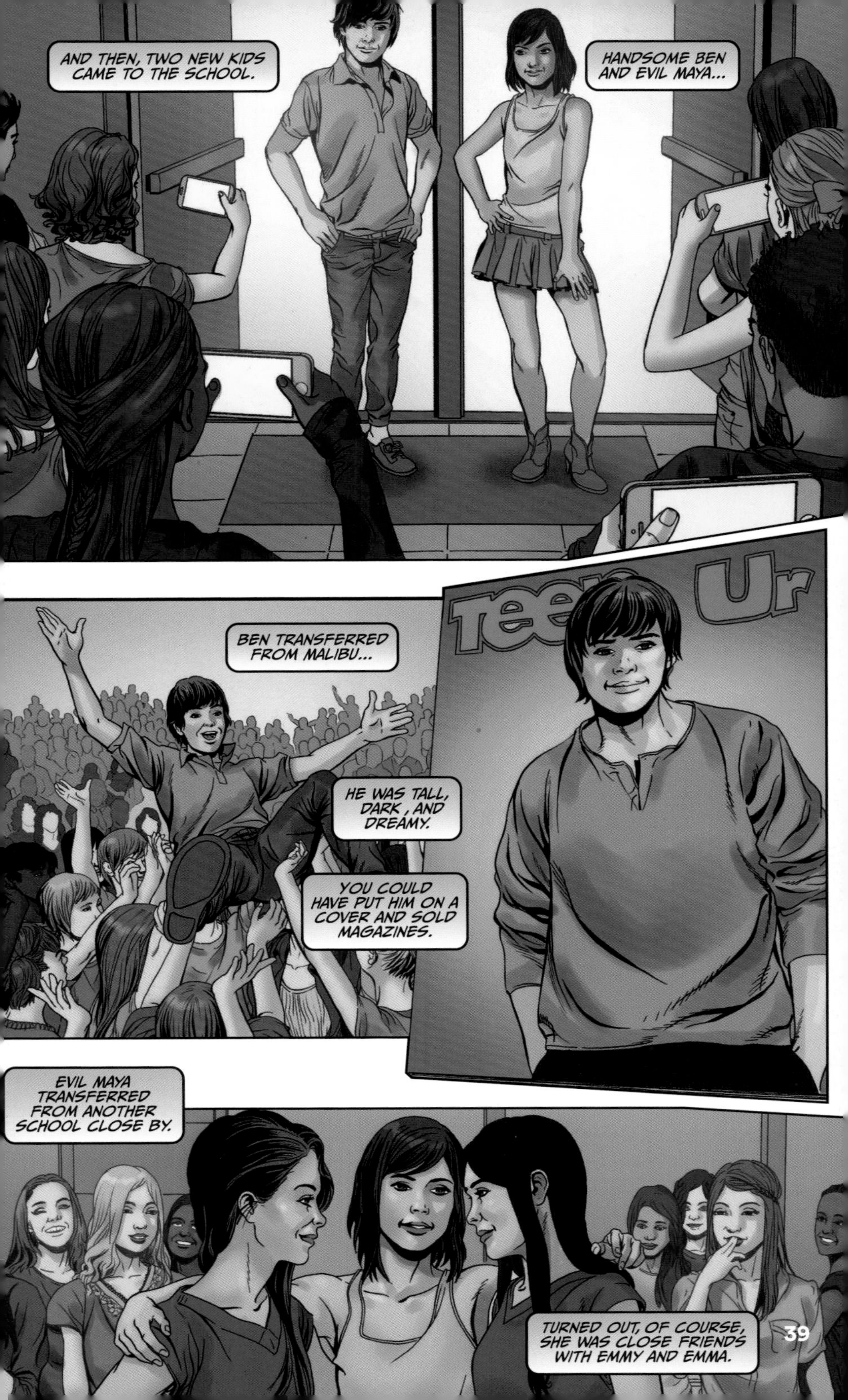
AND THEN, TWO NEW KIDS CAME TO THE SCHOOL.
HANDSOME BEN AND EVIL MAYA...
BEN TRANSFERRED FROM MALIBU...
HE WAS TALL, DARK, AND DREAMY.
YOU COULD HAVE PUT HIM ON A COVER AND SOLD MAGAZINES.
EVIL MAYA TRANSFERRED FROM ANOTHER SCHOOL CLOSE BY.
TURNED OUT, OF COURSE, SHE WAS CLOSE FRIENDS WITH EMMY AND EMMA.

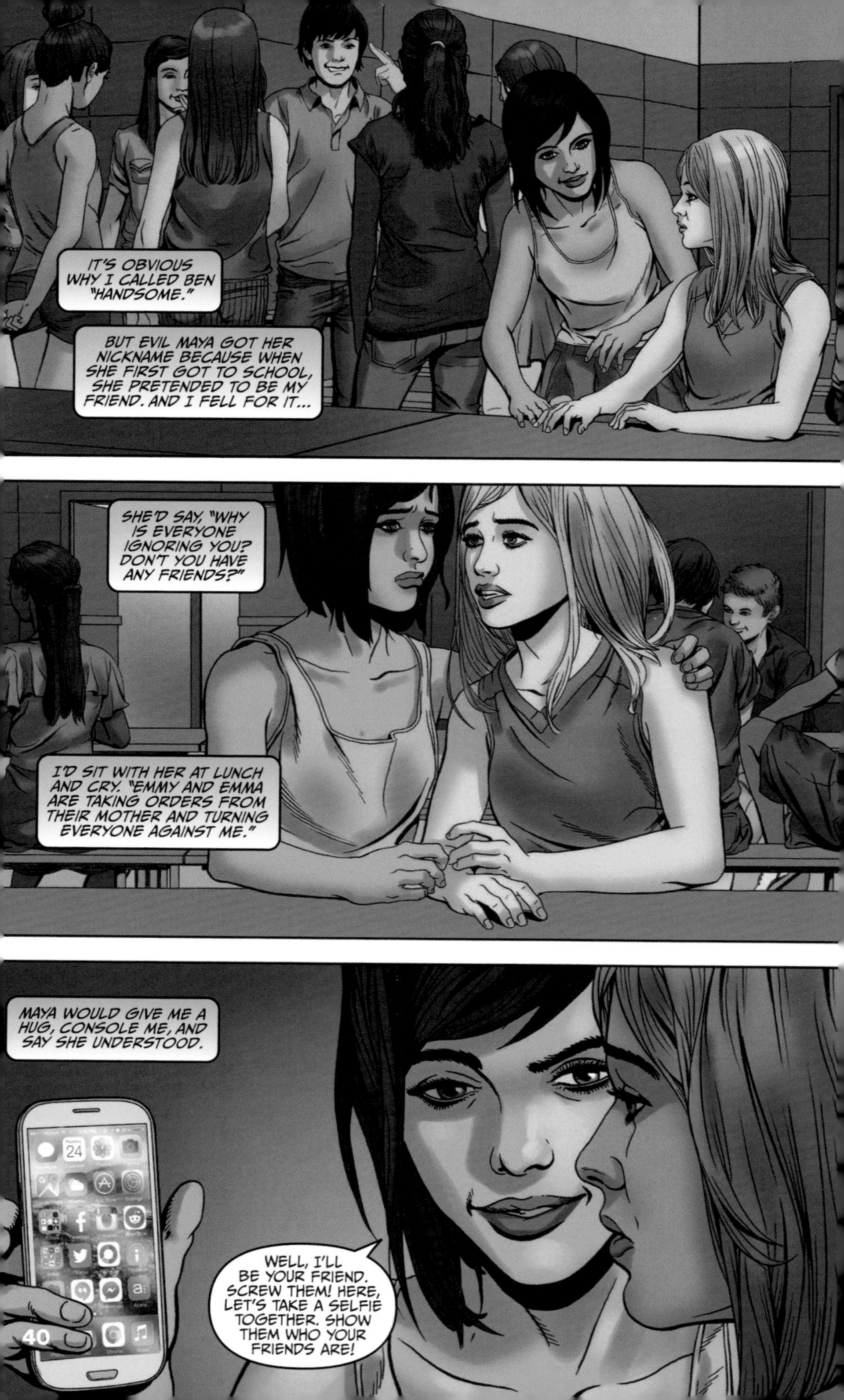
IT'S OBVIOUS WHY I CALLED BEN "HANDSOME."
BUT EVIL MAYA GOT HER NICKNAME BECAUSE WHEN SHE FIRST GOT TO SCHOOL, SHE PRETENDED TO BE MY FRIEND. AND I FELL FOR IT...
SHE'D SAY, "WHY IS EVERYONE IGNORING YOU? DON'T YOU HAVE ANY FRIENDS?"
I'D SIT WITH HER AT LUNCH AND CRY. "EMMY AND EMMA ARE TAKING ORDERS FROM THEIR MOTHER AND TURNING EVERYONE AGAINST ME."
MAYA WOULD GIVE ME A HUG, CONSOLE ME, AND SAY SHE UNDERSTOOD.
24
WELL, I'LL BE YOUR FRIEND. SCREW THEM! HERE, LET'S TAKE A SELFIE TOGETHER. SHOW THEM WHO YOUR FRIENDS ARE!

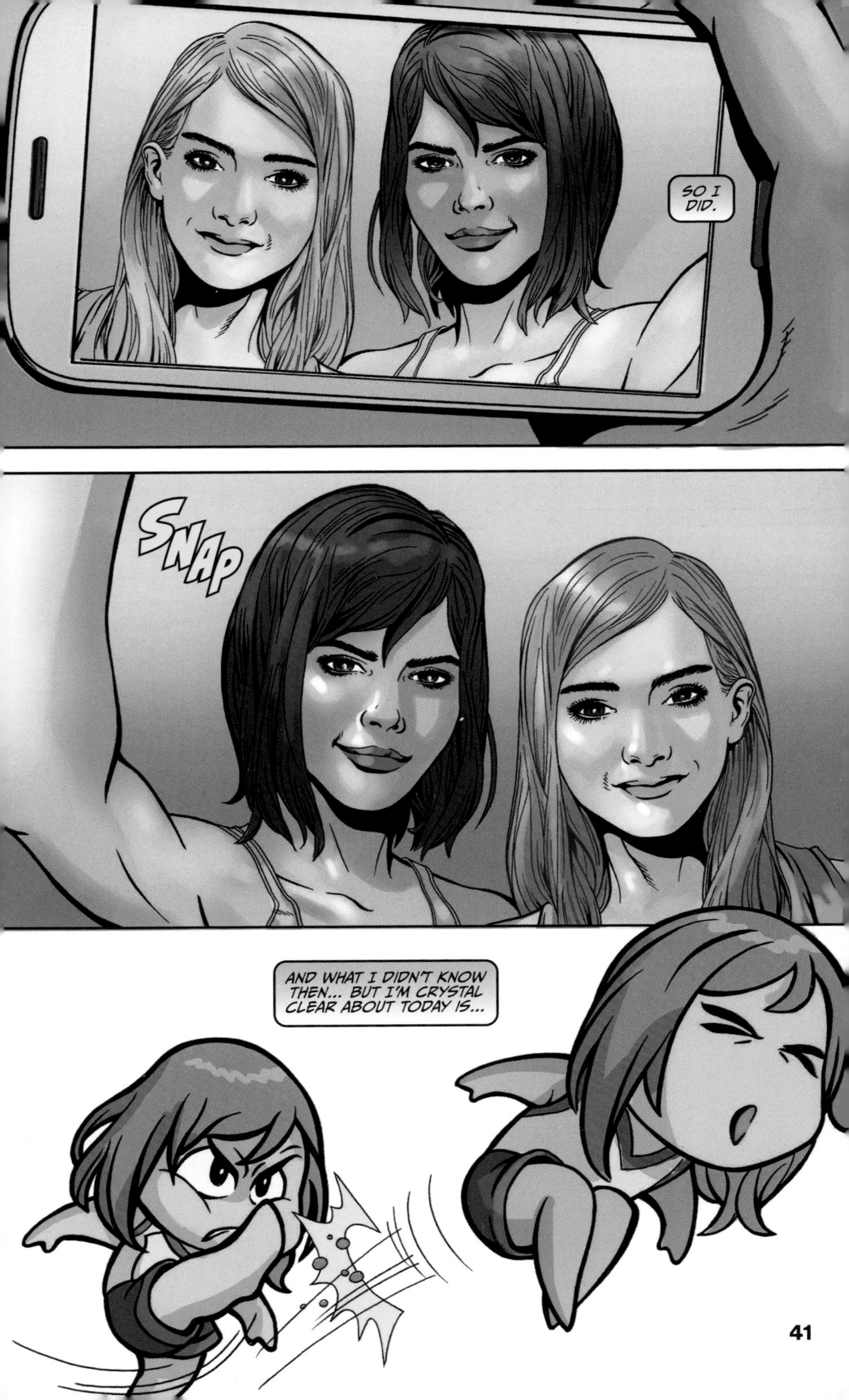
SO I DID.
SNAP
AND WHAT I DIDN'T KNOW THEN... BUT I'M CRYSTAL CLEAR ABOUT TODAY IS...

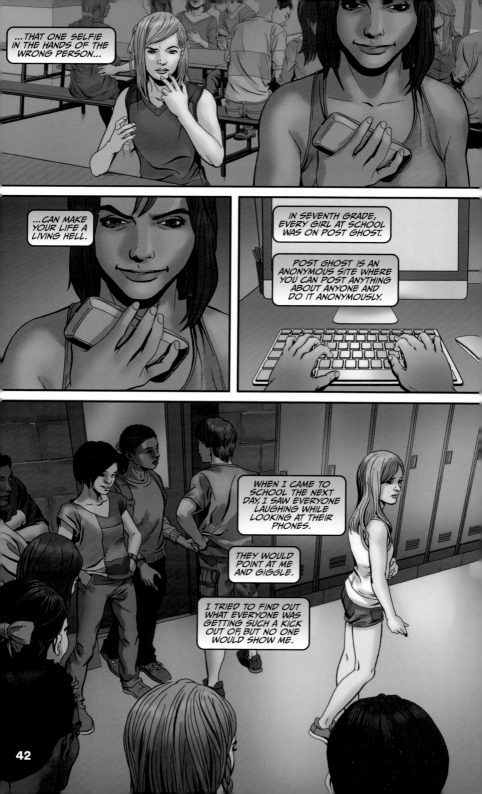

...THAT ONE SELFIE IN THE HANDS OF THE WRONG PERSON...

...CAN MAKE YOUR LIFE A LIVING HELL.

IN SEVENTH GRADE, EVERY GIRL AT SCHOOL WAS ON POST GHOST.

POST GHOST IS AN ANONYMOUS SITE WHERE YOU CAN POST ANYTHING ABOUT ANYONE AND DO IT ANONYMOUSLY.

WHEN I CAME TO SCHOOL THE NEXT DAY, I SAW EVERYONE LAUGHING WHILE LOOKING AT THEIR PHONES.

THEY WOULD POINT AT ME AND GIGGLE.

I TRIED TO FIND OUT WHAT EVERYONE WAS GETTING SUCH A KICK OUT OF, BUT NO ONE WOULD SHOW ME.

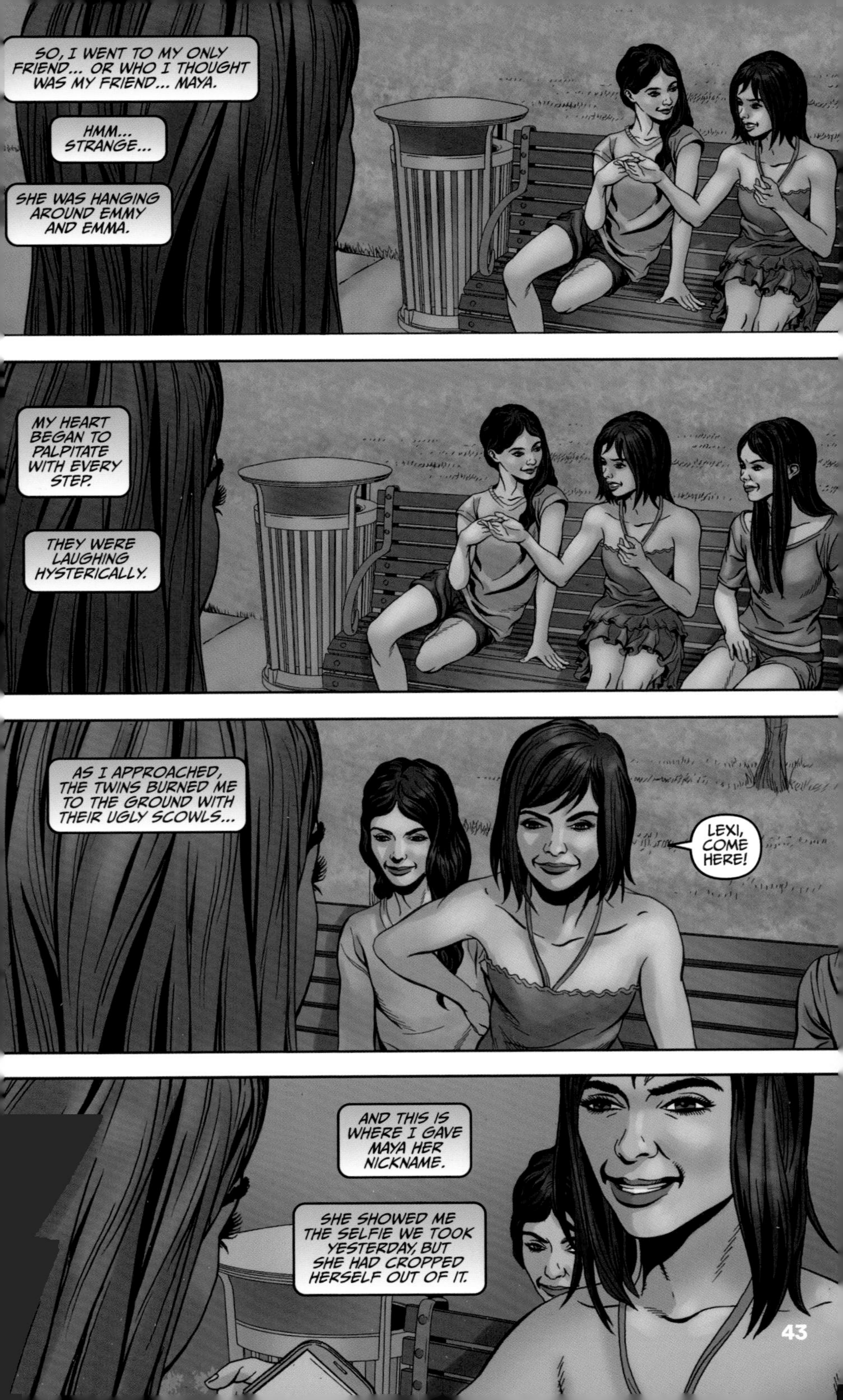
SO, I WENT TO MY ONLY FRIEND... OR WHO I THOUGHT WAS MY FRIEND... MAYA.
HMM... STRANGE...
SHE WAS HANGING AROUND EMMY AND EMMA.
MY HEART BEGAN TO PALPITATE WITH EVERY STEP.
THEY WERE LAUGHING HYSTERICALLY.
AS I APPROACHED, THE TWINS BURNED ME TO THE GROUND WITH THEIR UGLY SCOWLS...
LEXI, COME HERE!
AND THIS IS WHERE I GAVE MAYA HER NICKNAME.
SHE SHOWED ME THE SELFIE WE TOOK YESTERDAY, BUT SHE HAD CROPPED HERSELF OUT OF IT.

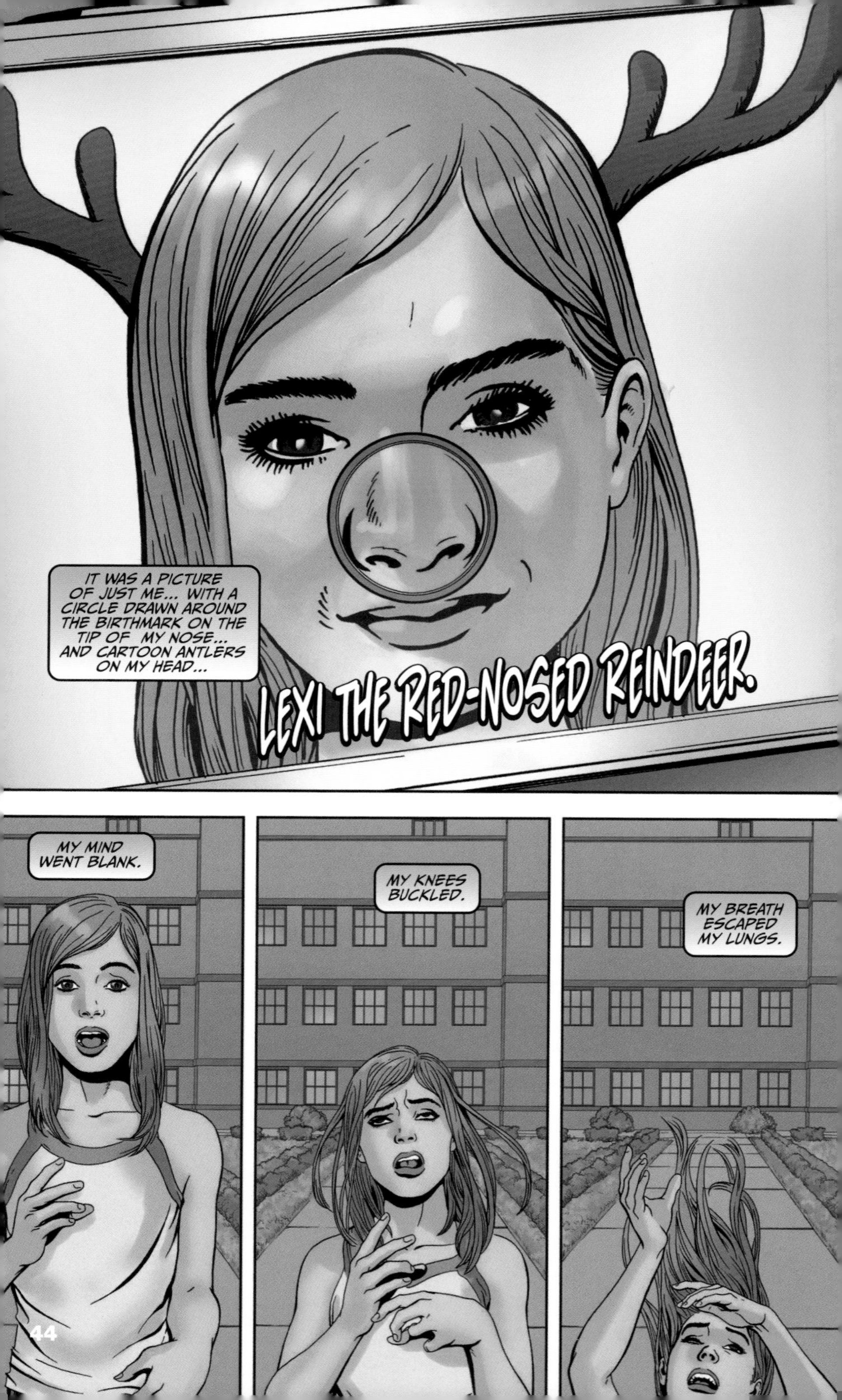
IT WAS A PICTURE OF JUST ME... WITH A CIRCLE DRAWN AROUND THE BIRTHMARK ON THE TIP OF MY NOSE... AND CARTOON ANTLERS ON MY HEAD...
LEXI THE RED-NOSED REINDEER.
MY MIND WENT BLANK.
MY KNEES BUCKLED.
MY BREATH ESCAPED MY LUNGS.

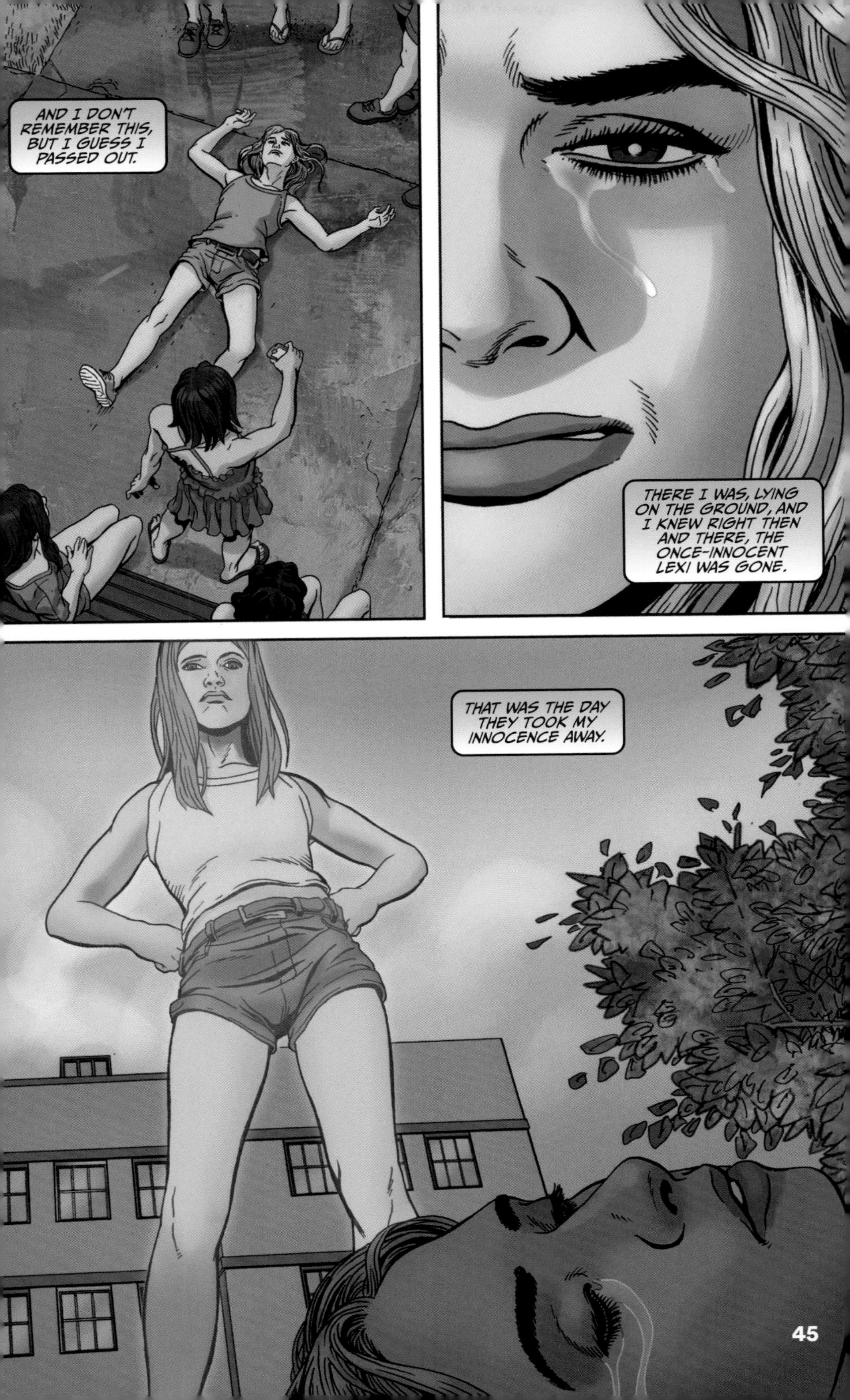

AND I DON'T REMEMBER THIS, BUT I GUESS I PASSED OUT.
THERE I WAS, LYING ON THE GROUND, AND I KNEW RIGHT THEN AND THERE, THE ONCE-INNOCENT LEXI WAS GONE.
THAT WAS THE DAY THEY TOOK MY INNOCENCE AWAY.

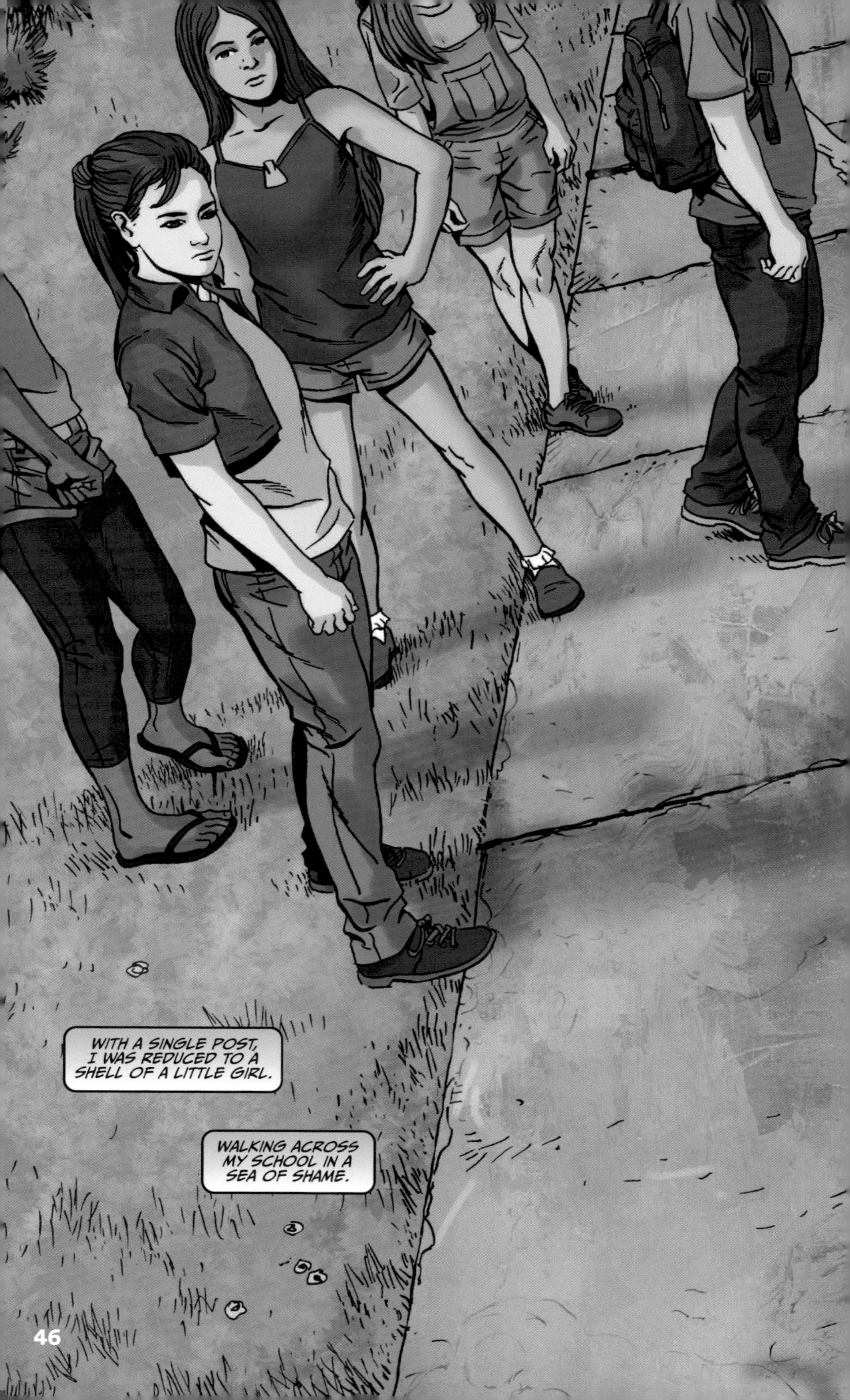
WITH A SINGLE POST, I WAS REDUCED TO A SHELL OF A LITTLE GIRL.
WALKING ACROSS MY SCHOOL IN A SEA OF SHAME.

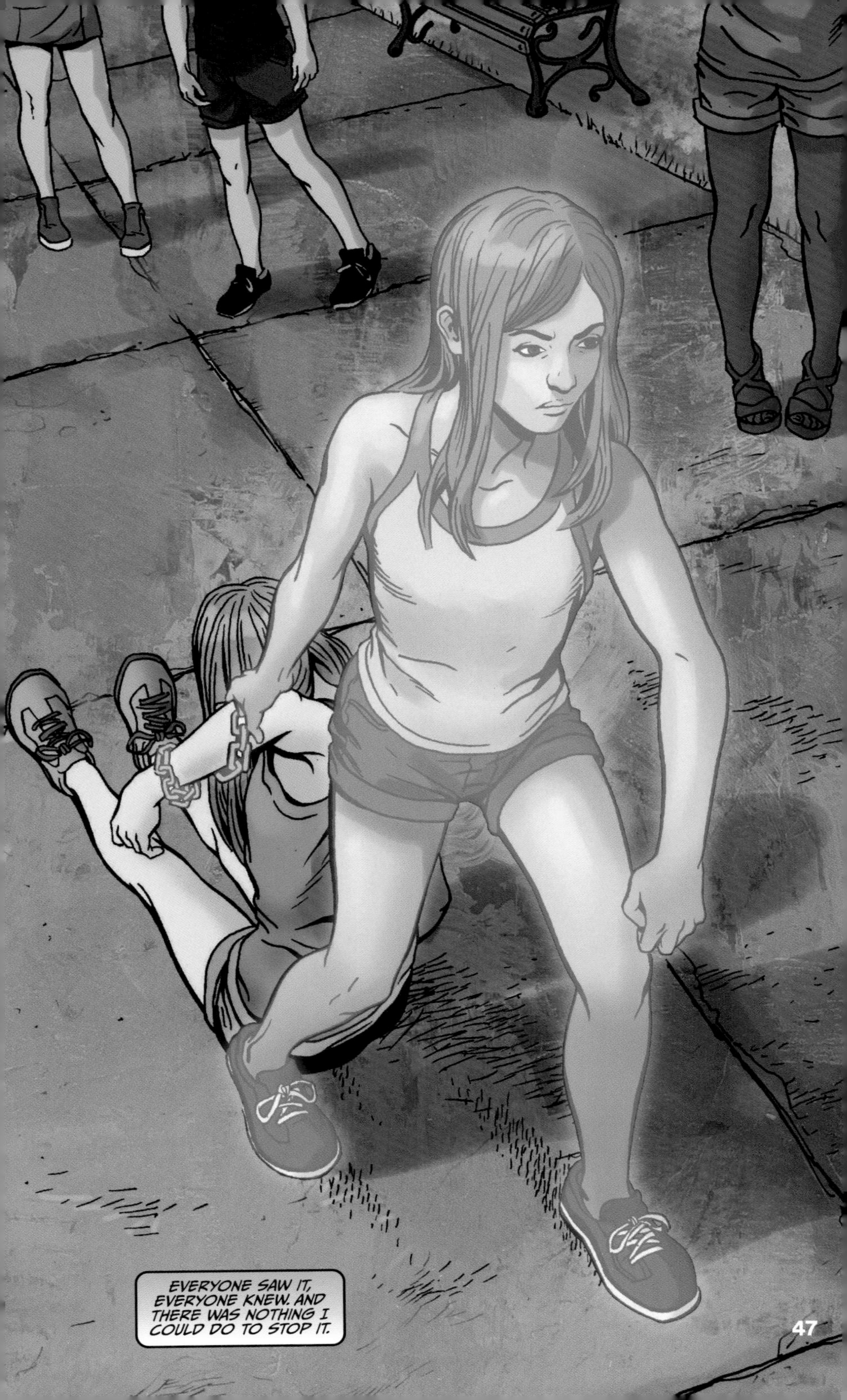
EVERYONE SAW IT, EVERYONE KNEW. AND THERE WAS NOTHING I COULD DO TO STOP IT.

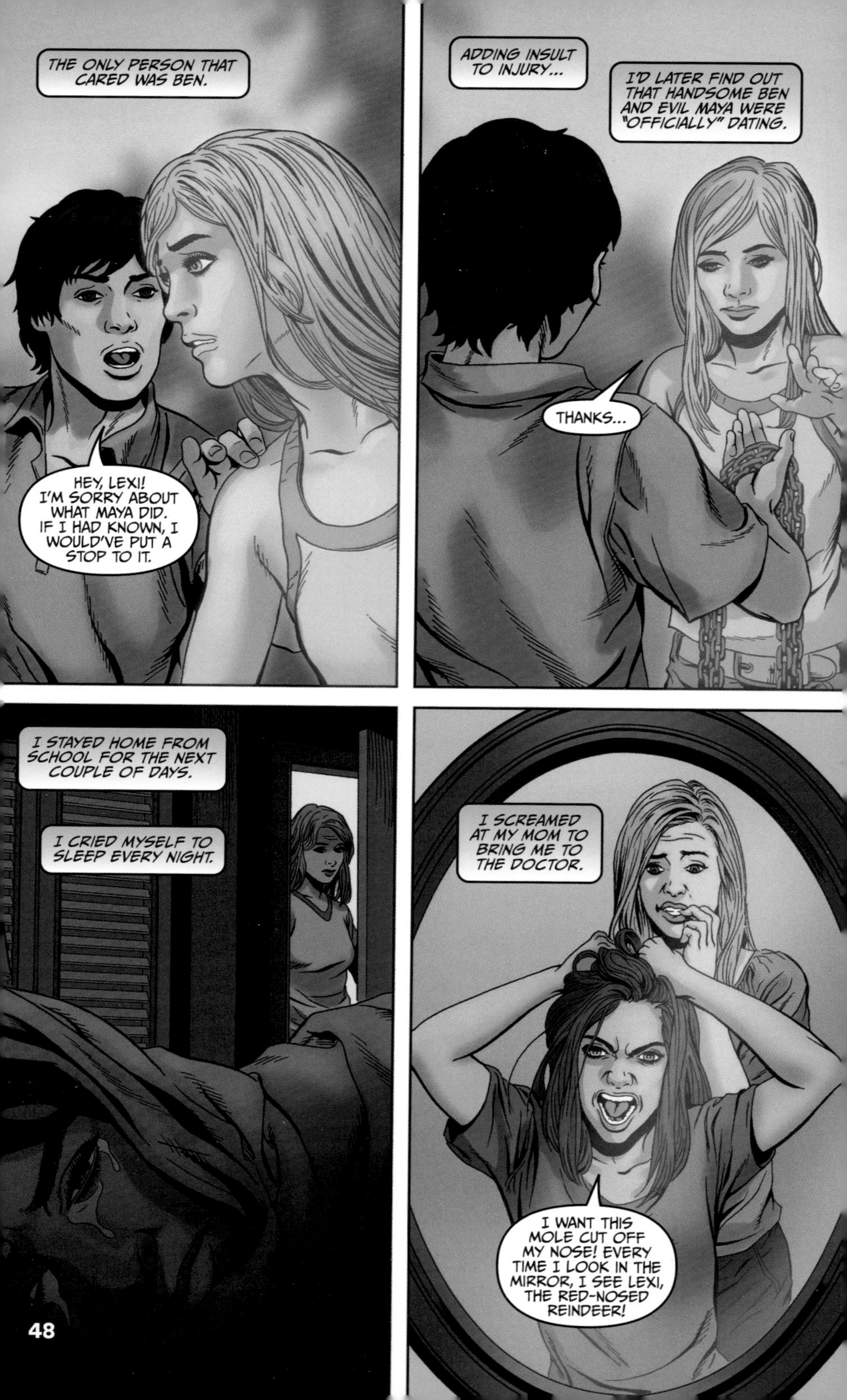
THE ONLY PERSON THAT CARED WAS BEN.
HEY, LEXI! I'M SORRY ABOUT WHAT MAYA DID. IF I HAD KNOWN, I WOULD'VE PUT A STOP TO IT.
ADDING INSULT TO INJURY...
I'D LATER FIND OUT THAT HANDSOME BEN AND EVIL MAYA WERE "OFFICIALLY" DATING.
THANKS...
I STAYED HOME FROM SCHOOL FOR THE NEXT COUPLE OF DAYS.
I CRIED MYSELF TO SLEEP EVERY NIGHT.
I SCREAMED AT MY MOM TO BRING ME TO THE DOCTOR.
I WANT THIS MOLE CUT OFF MY NOSE! EVERY TIME I LOOK IN THE MIRROR, I SEE LEXI, THE RED-NOSED REINDEER!

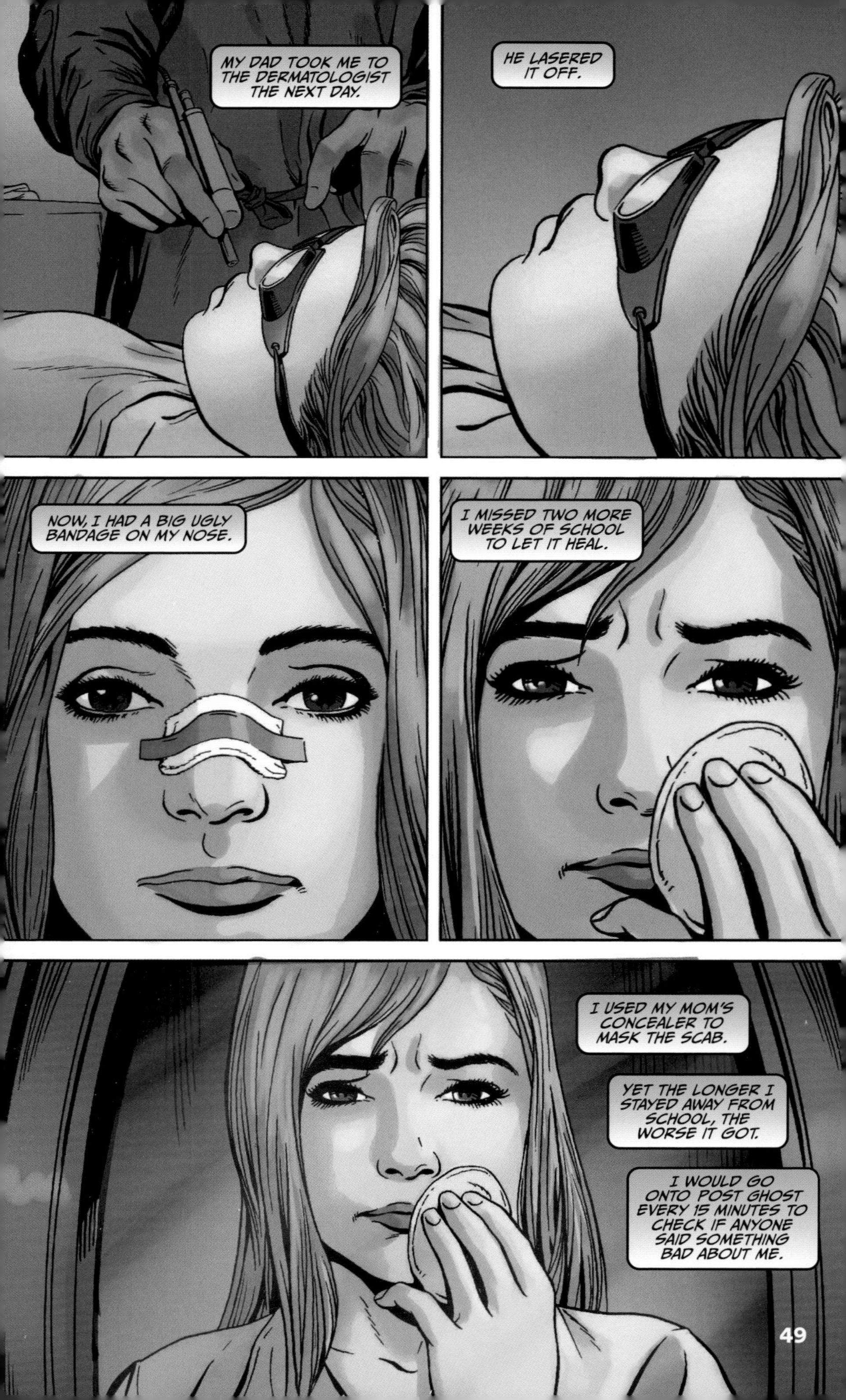
MY DAD TOOK ME TO THE DERMATOLOGIST THE NEXT DAY.
HE LASERED IT OFF.
NOW, I HAD A BIG UGLY BANDAGE ON MY NOSE.
I MISSED TWO MORE WEEKS OF SCHOOL TO LET IT HEAL.
I USED MY MOM'S CONCEALER TO MASK THE SCAB.
YET THE LONGER I STAYED AWAY FROM SCHOOL, THE WORSE IT GOT.
I WOULD GO ONTO POST GHOST EVERY 15 MINUTES TO CHECK IF ANYONE SAID SOMETHING BAD ABOUT ME.

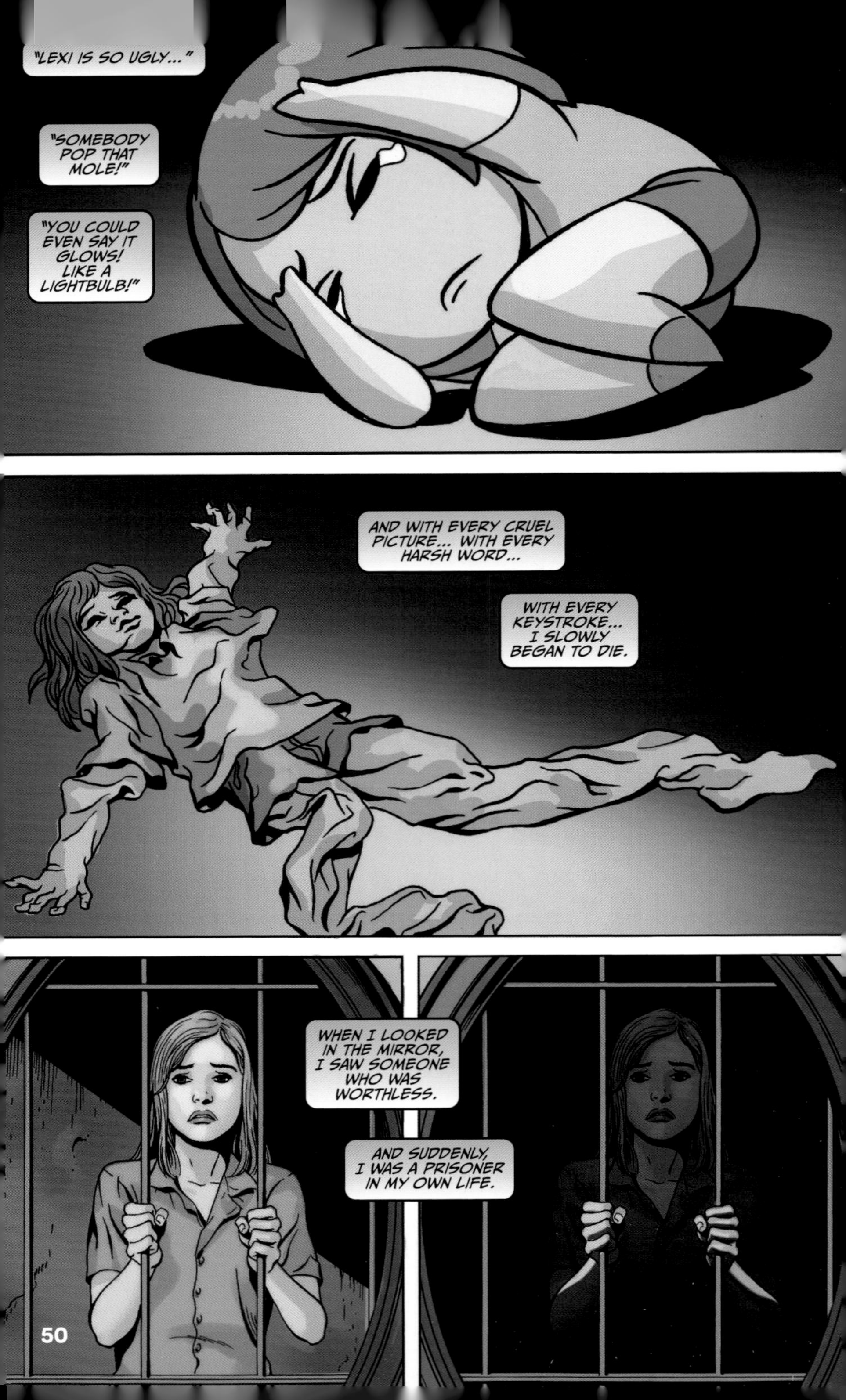
"LEXI IS SO UGLY..."
"SOMEBODY POP THAT MOLE!"
"YOU COULD EVEN SAY IT GLOWS! LIKE A LIGHTBULB!"
AND WITH EVERY CRUEL PICTURE... WITH EVERY HARSH WORD...
WITH EVERY KEYSTROKE... I SLOWLY BEGAN TO DIE.
WHEN I LOOKED IN THE MIRROR, I SAW SOMEONE WHO WAS WORTHLESS.
AND SUDDENLY, I WAS A PRISONER IN MY OWN LIFE.

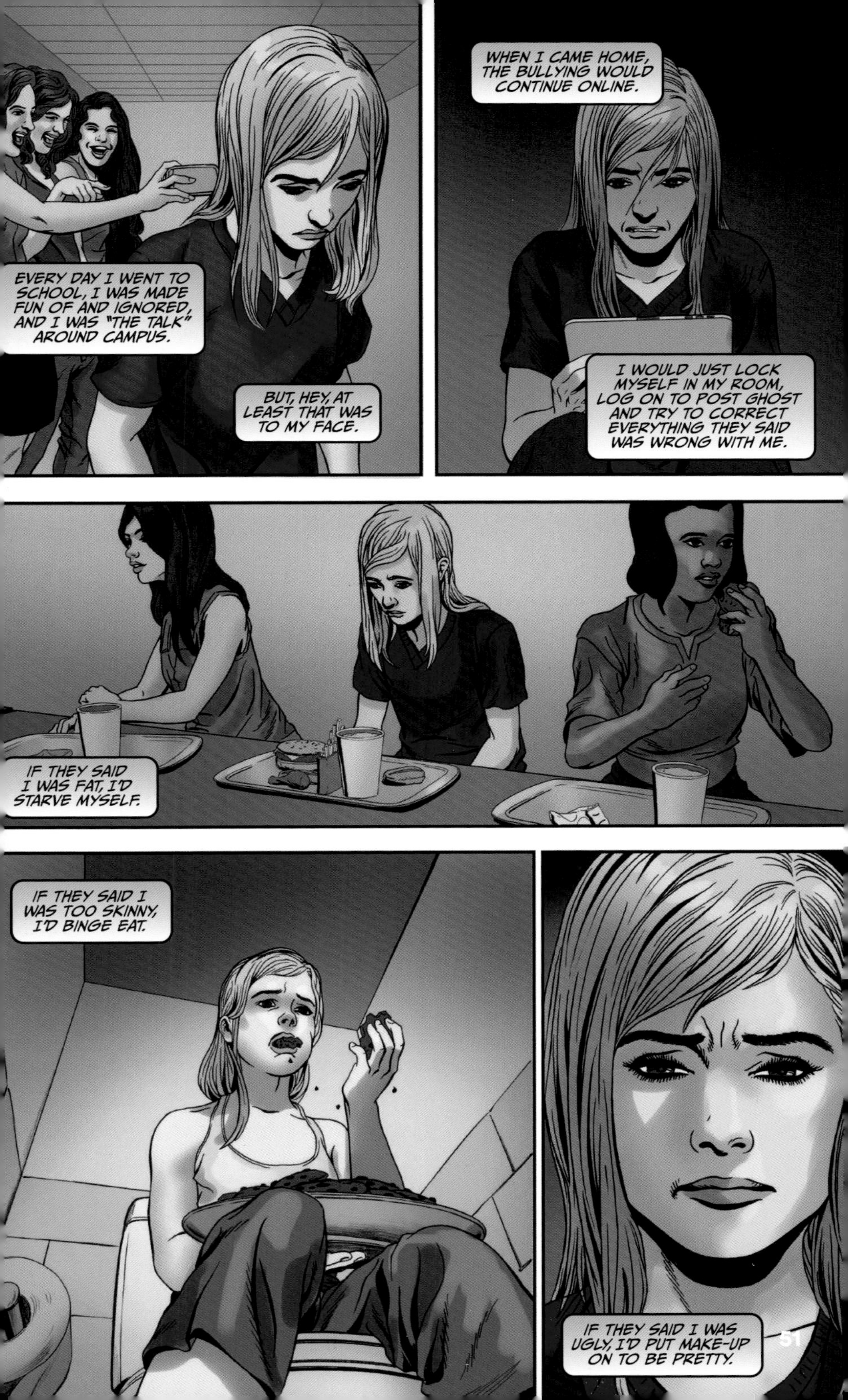
EVERY DAY I WENT TO SCHOOL, I WAS MADE FUN OF AND IGNORED, AND I WAS "THE TALK" AROUND CAMPUS.
BUT, HEY, AT LEAST THAT WAS TO MY FACE.
WHEN I CAME HOME, THE BULLYING WOULD CONTINUE ONLINE.
I WOULD JUST LOCK MYSELF IN MY ROOM, LOG ON TO POST GHOST AND TRY TO CORRECT EVERYTHING THEY SAID WAS WRONG WITH ME.
IF THEY SAID I WAS FAT, I'D STARVE MYSELF.
IF THEY SAID I WAS TOO SKINNY, I'D BINGE EAT.
IF THEY SAID I WAS UGLY, I'D PUT MAKE-UP ON TO BE PRETTY.

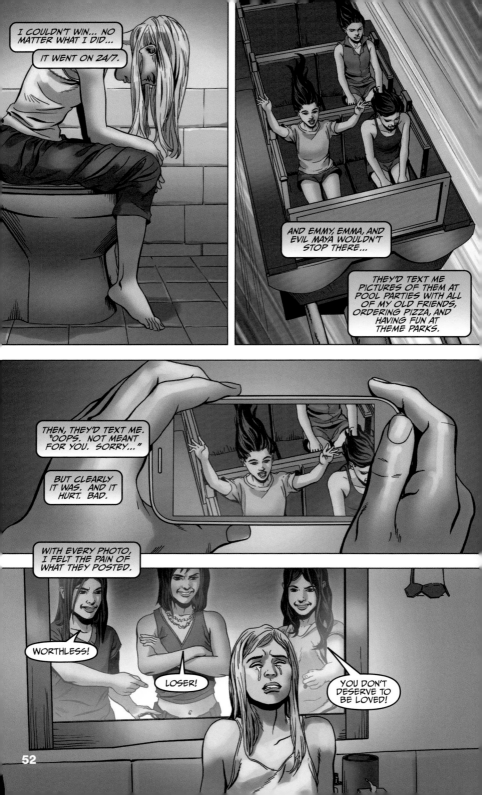

I COULDN'T WIN... NO MATTER WHAT I DID...

IT WENT ON 24/7.

AND EMMY, EMMA, AND EVIL MAYA WOULDN'T STOP THERE...

THEY'D TEXT ME PICTURES OF THEM AT POOL PARTIES WITH ALL OF MY OLD FRIENDS, ORDERING PIZZA, AND HAVING FUN AT THEME PARKS.

THEN, THEY'D TEXT ME. "OOPS. NOT MEANT FOR YOU. SORRY..."

BUT CLEARLY IT WAS. AND IT HURT. BAD.

WITH EVERY PHOTO, I FELT THE PAIN OF WHAT THEY POSTED.

WORTHLESS!

LOSER!

YOU DON'T DESERVE TO BE LOVED!

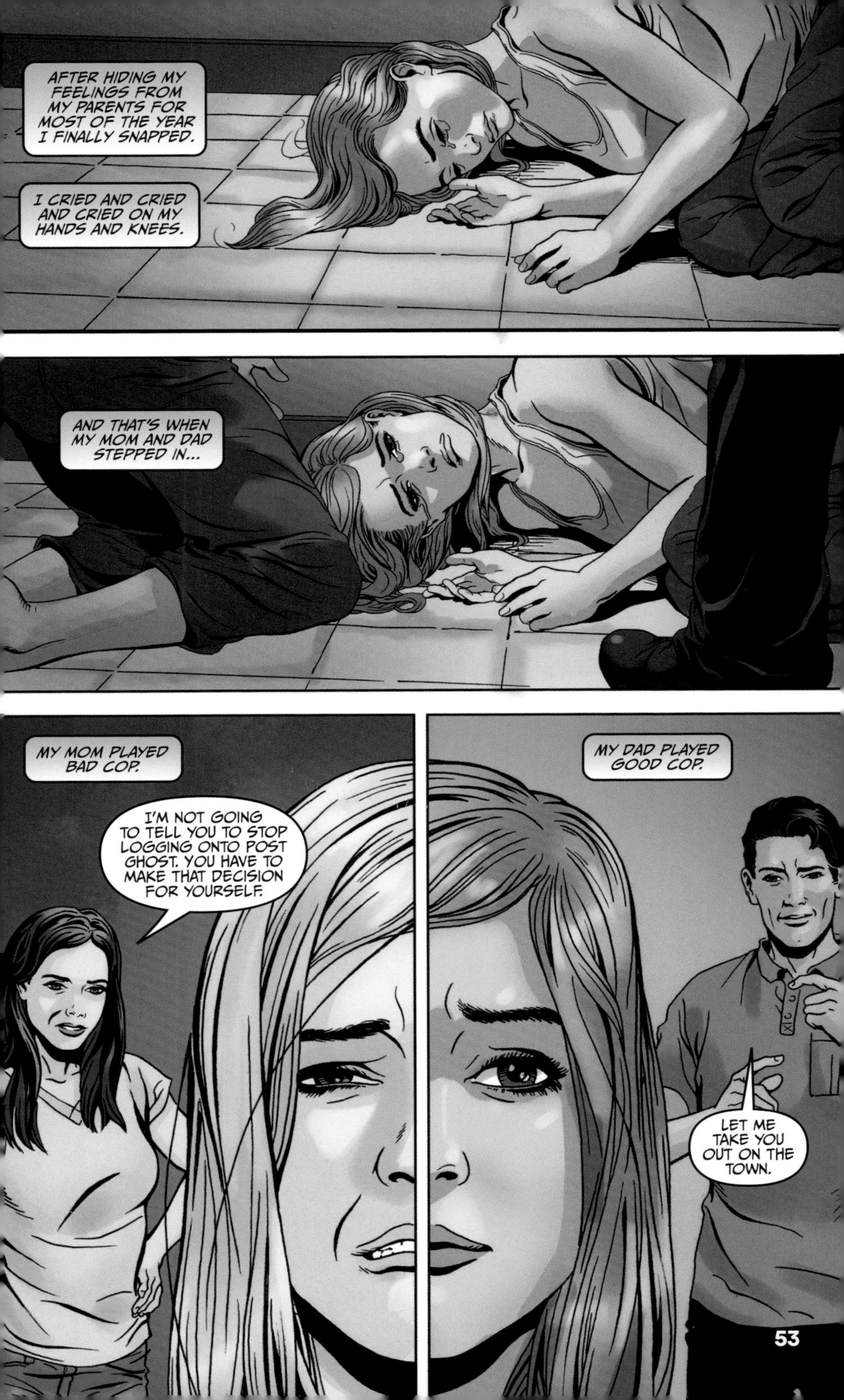
AFTER HIDING MY FEELINGS FROM MY PARENTS FOR MOST OF THE YEAR I FINALLY SNAPPED.
I CRIED AND CRIED AND CRIED ON MY HANDS AND KNEES.
AND THAT'S WHEN MY MOM AND DAD STEPPED IN...
MY MOM PLAYED BAD COP.
I'M NOT GOING TO TELL YOU TO STOP LOGGING ONTO POST GHOST. YOU HAVE TO MAKE THAT DECISION FOR YOURSELF.
MY DAD PLAYED GOOD COP.
LET ME TAKE YOU OUT ON THE TOWN.

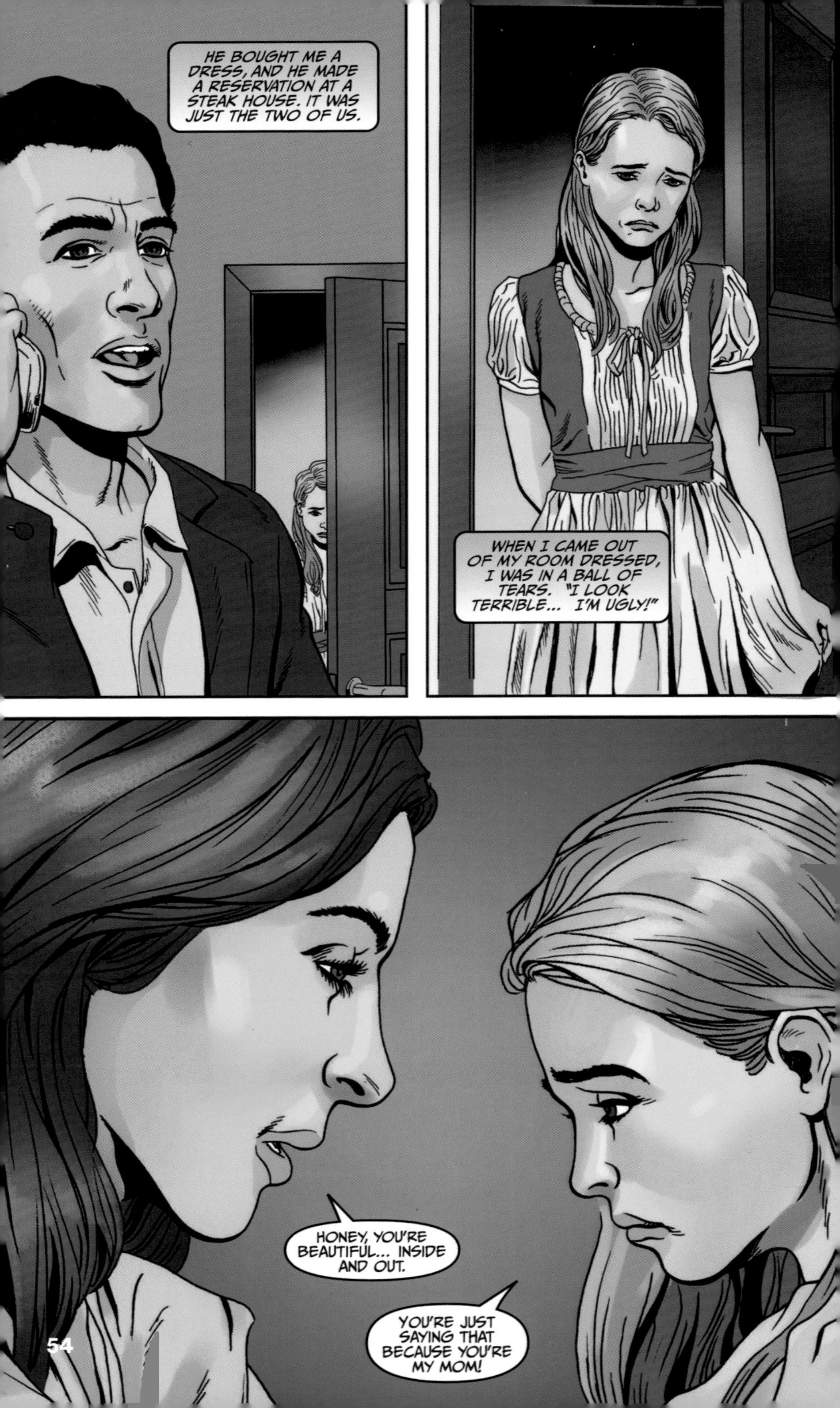
HE BOUGHT ME A DRESS, AND HE MADE A RESERVATION AT A STEAK HOUSE. IT WAS JUST THE TWO OF US.
WHEN I CAME OUT OF MY ROOM DRESSED, I WAS IN A BALL OF TEARS. "I LOOK TERRIBLE... I'M UGLY!"
HONEY, YOU'RE BEAUTIFUL... INSIDE AND OUT.
YOU'RE JUST SAYING THAT BECAUSE YOU'RE MY MOM!

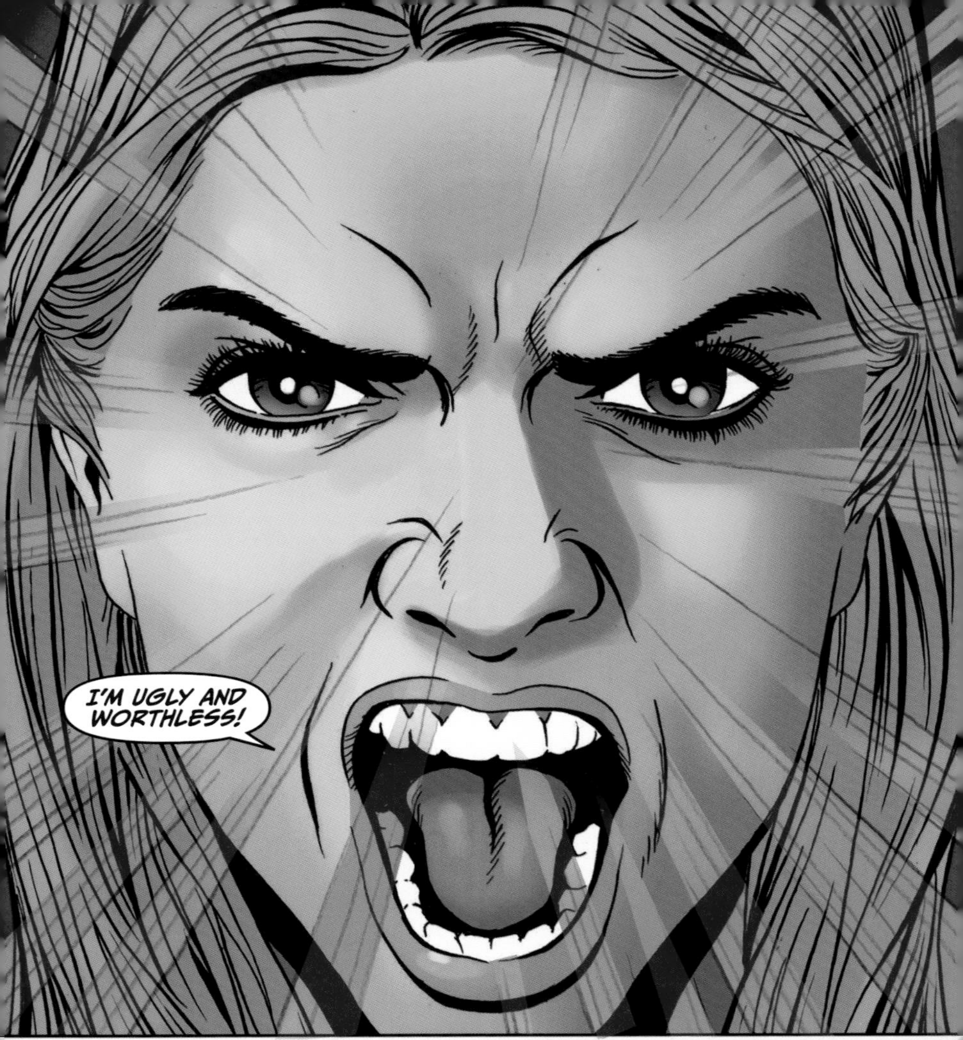
I'M UGLY AND WORTHLESS!

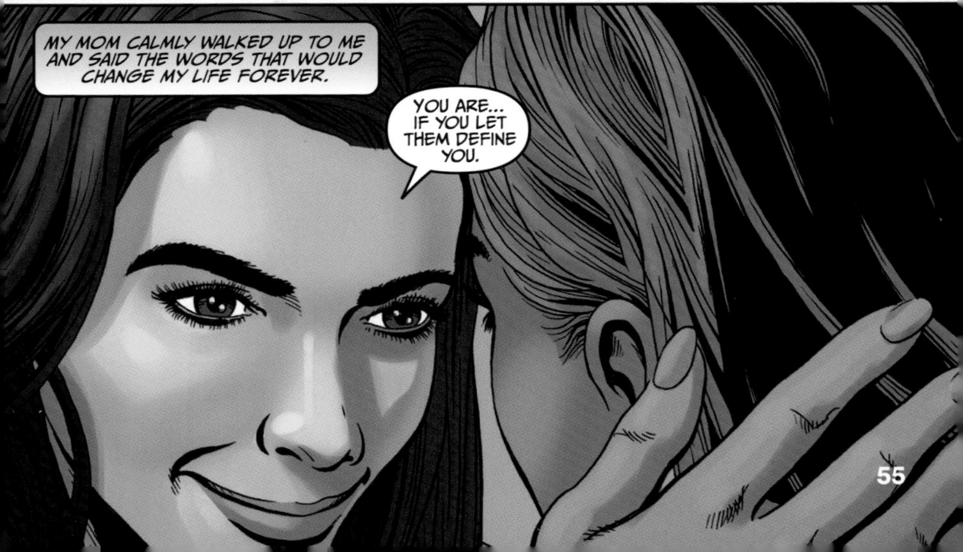
MY MOM CALMLY WALKED UP TO ME AND SAID THE WORDS THAT WOULD CHANGE MY LIFE FOREVER.
YOU ARE... IF YOU LET THEM DEFINE YOU.

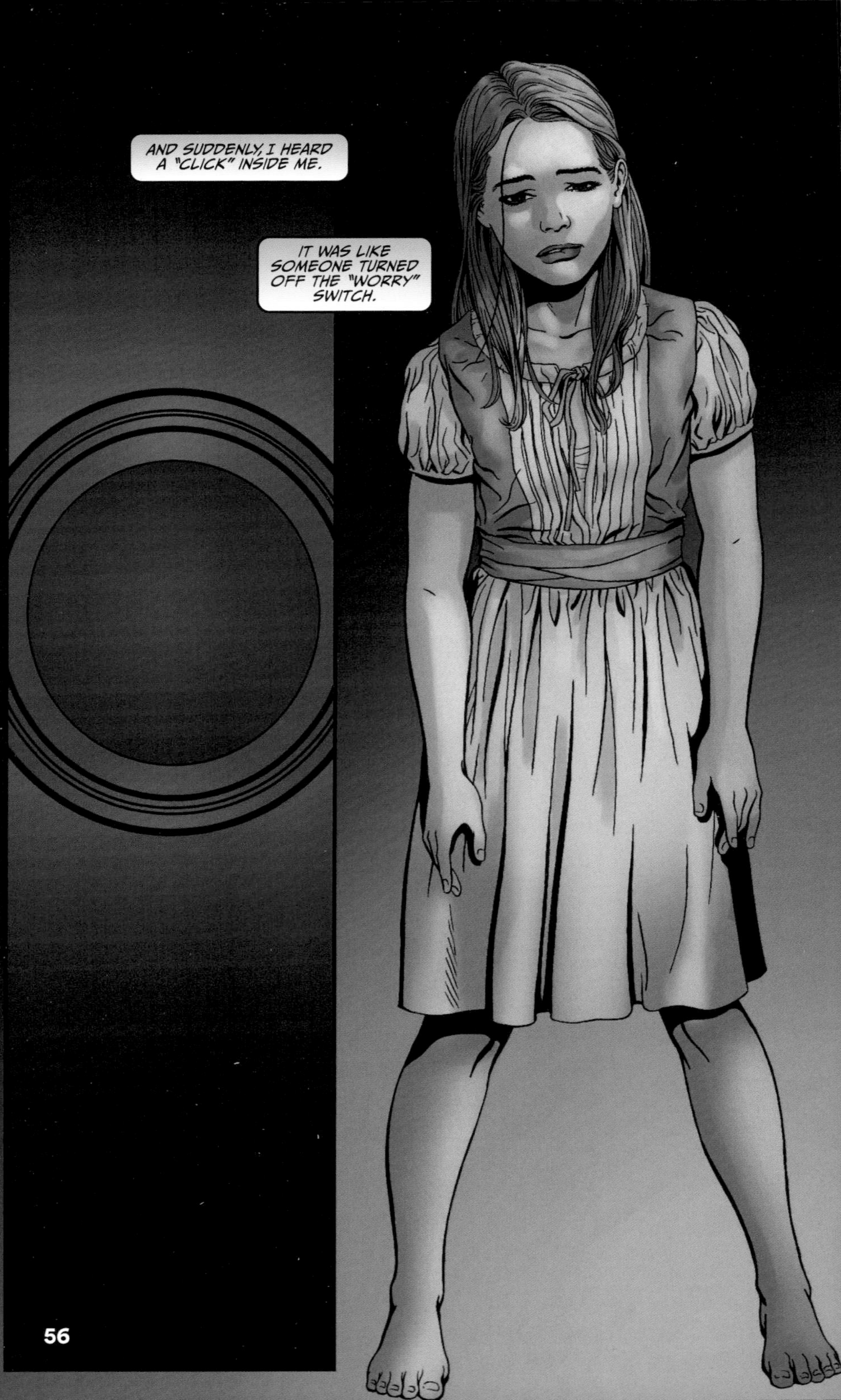
AND SUDDENLY, I HEARD A "CLICK" INSIDE ME.
IT WAS LIKE SOMEONE TURNED OFF THE "WORRY" SWITCH.

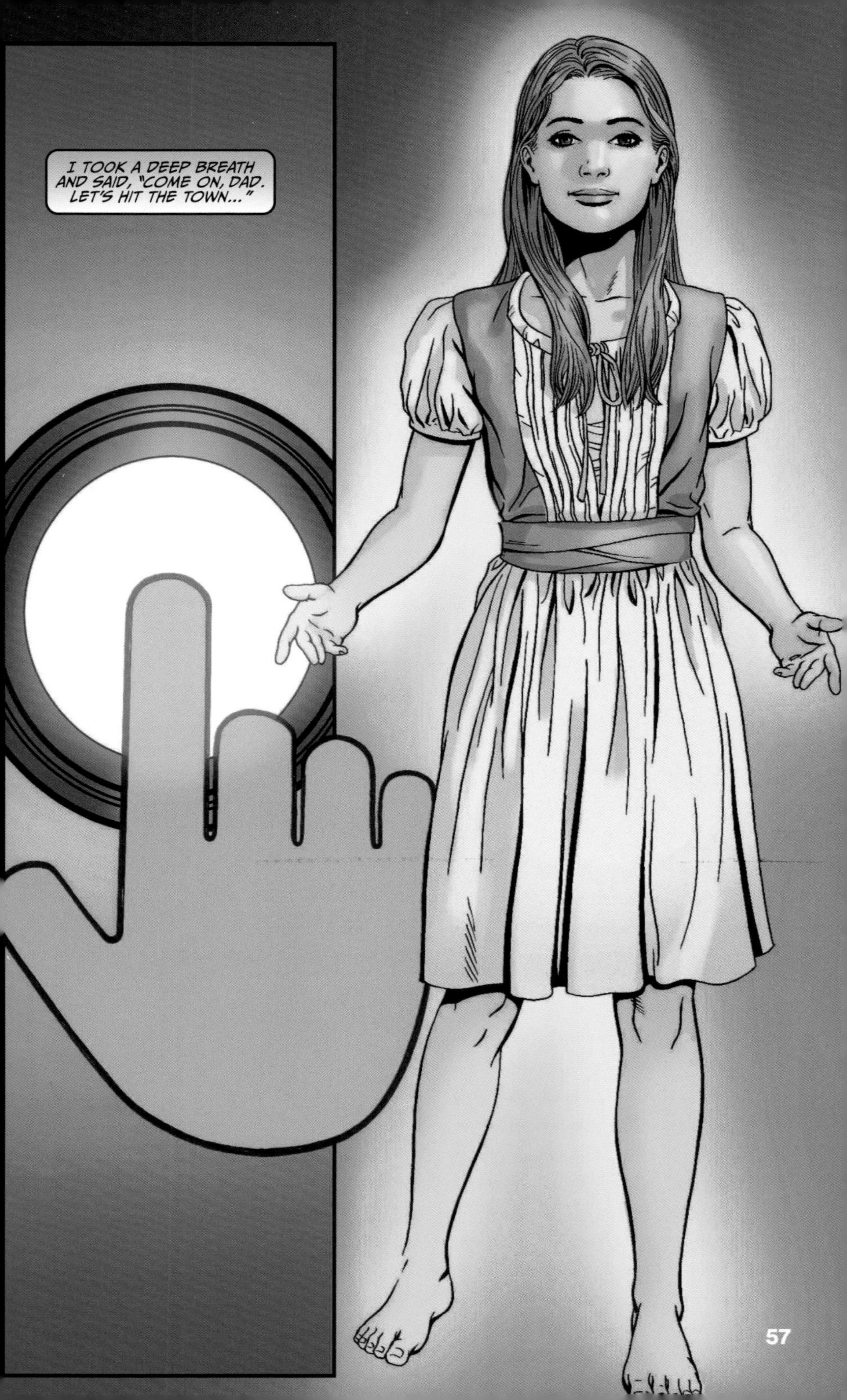
I TOOK A DEEP BREATH AND SAID, "COME ON, DAD. LET'S HIT THE TOWN..."

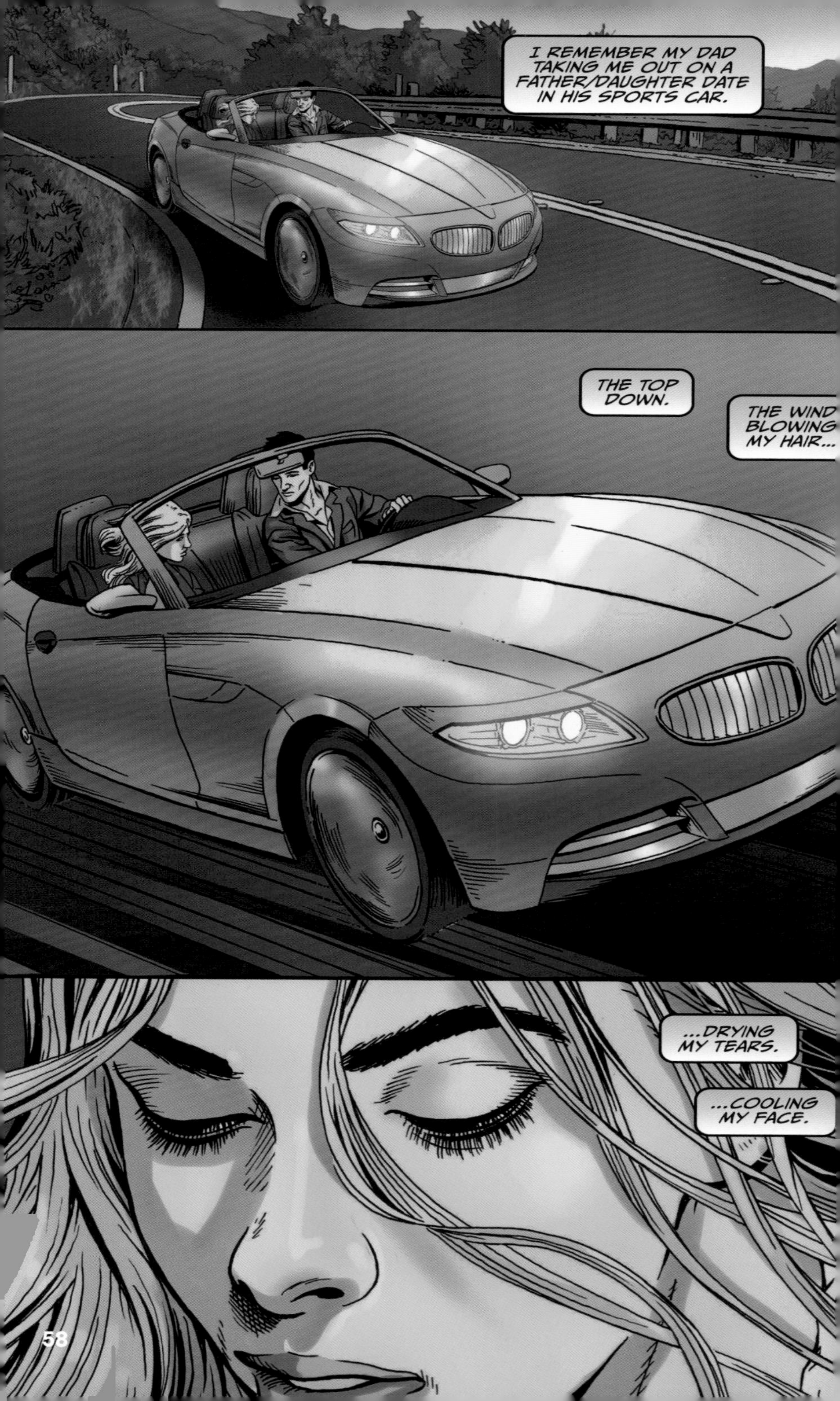

I REMEMBER MY DAD TAKING ME OUT ON A FATHER/DAUGHTER DATE IN HIS SPORTS CAR.
THE TOP DOWN.
THE WIND BLOWING MY HAIR...
...DRYING MY TEARS.
...COOLING MY FACE.

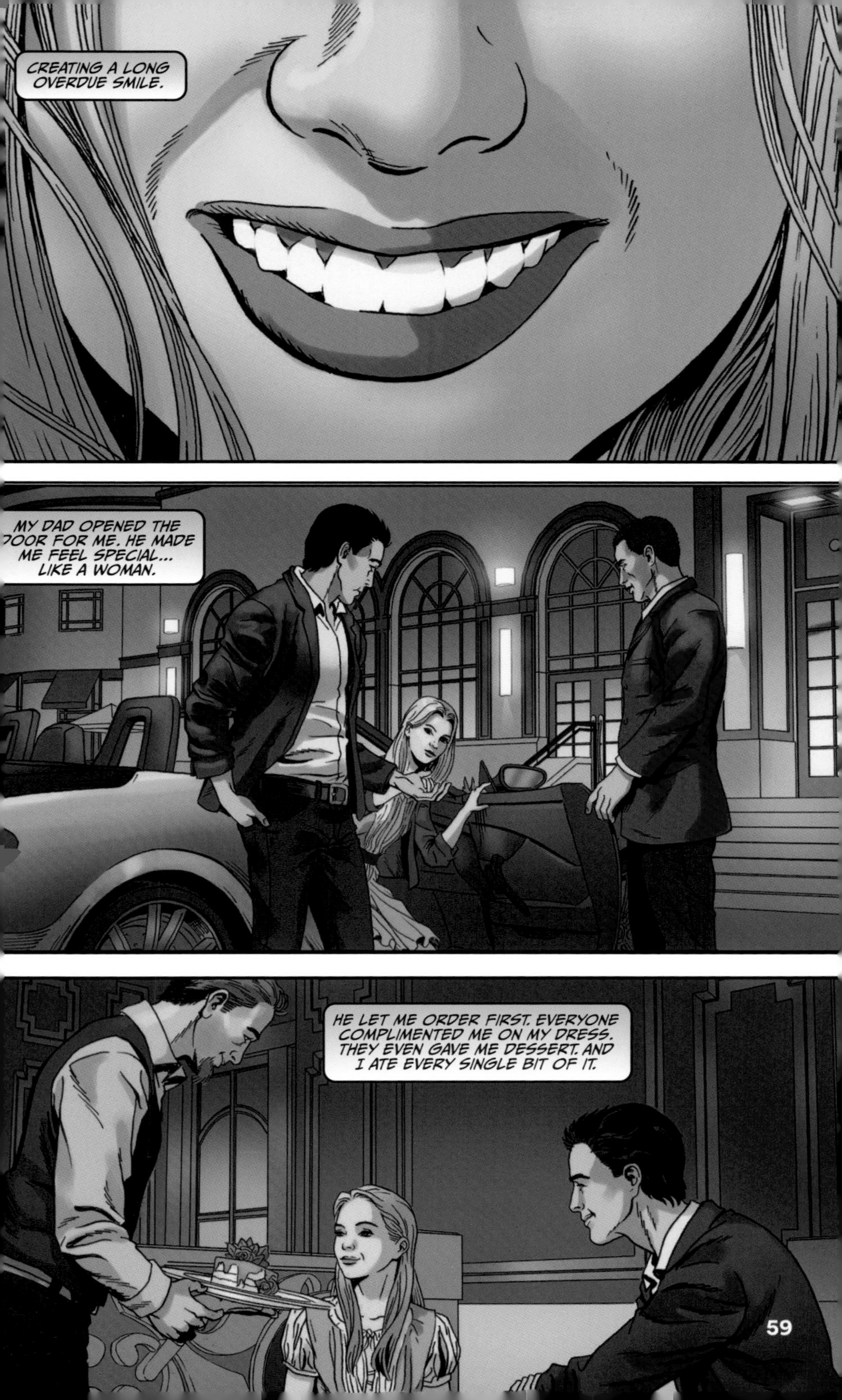
CREATING A LONG OVERDUE SMILE.
MY DAD OPENED THE DOOR FOR ME. HE MADE ME FEEL SPECIAL... LIKE A WOMAN.
HE LET ME ORDER FIRST. EVERYONE COMPLIMENTED ME ON MY DRESS. THEY EVEN GAVE ME DESSERT. AND I ATE EVERY SINGLE BIT OF IT.

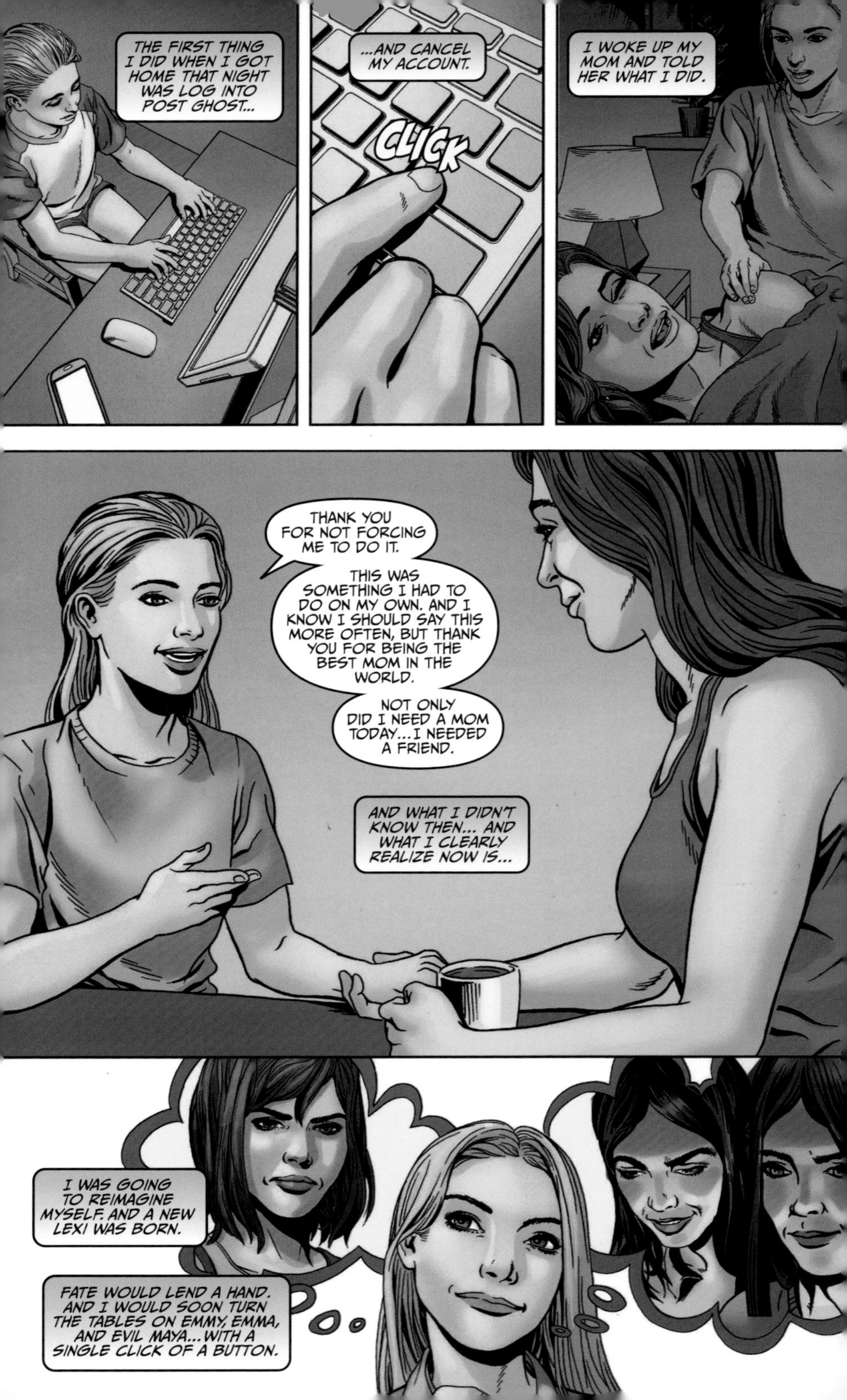
THE FIRST THING I DID WHEN I GOT HOME THAT NIGHT WAS LOG INTO POST GHOST...
...AND CANCEL MY ACCOUNT.
CLICK
I WOKE UP MY MOM AND TOLD HER WHAT I DID.
THANK YOU FOR NOT FORCING ME TO DO IT.
THIS WAS SOMETHING I HAD TO DO ON MY OWN. AND I KNOW I SHOULD SAY THIS MORE OFTEN, BUT THANK YOU FOR BEING THE BEST MOM IN THE WORLD.
NOT ONLY DID I NEED A MOM TODAY... I NEEDED A FRIEND.
AND WHAT I DIDN'T KNOW THEN... AND WHAT I CLEARLY REALIZE NOW IS...
I WAS GOING TO REIMAGINE MYSELF. AND A NEW LEXI WAS BORN.
FATE WOULD LEND A HAND. AND I WOULD SOON TURN THE TABLES ON EMMY, EMMA, AND EVIL MAYA... WITH A SINGLE CLICK OF A BUTTON.

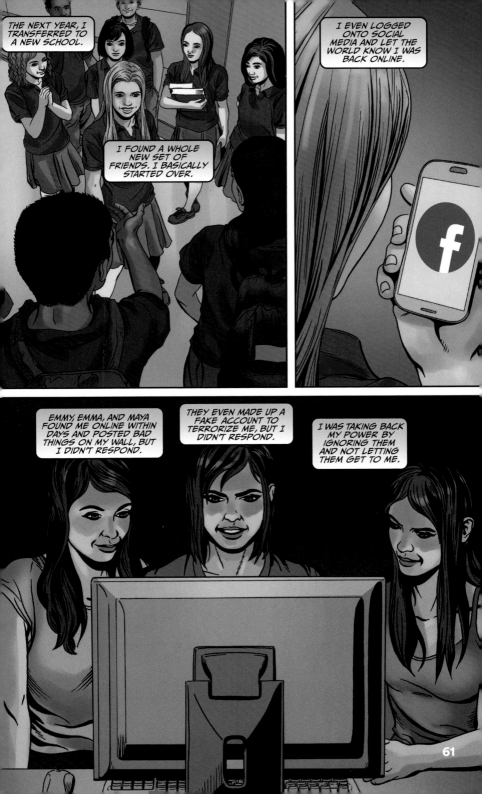

THE NEXT YEAR, I TRANSFERRED TO A NEW SCHOOL.

I FOUND A WHOLE NEW SET OF FRIENDS. I BASICALLY STARTED OVER.

I EVEN LOGGED ONTO SOCIAL MEDIA AND LET THE WORLD KNOW I WAS BACK ONLINE.

EMMY, EMMA, AND MAYA FOUND ME ONLINE WITHIN DAYS AND POSTED BAD THINGS ON MY WALL, BUT I DIDN'T RESPOND.

THEY EVEN MADE UP A FAKE ACCOUNT TO TERRORIZE ME, BUT I DIDN'T RESPOND.

I WAS TAKING BACK MY POWER BY IGNORING THEM AND NOT LETTING THEM GET TO ME.

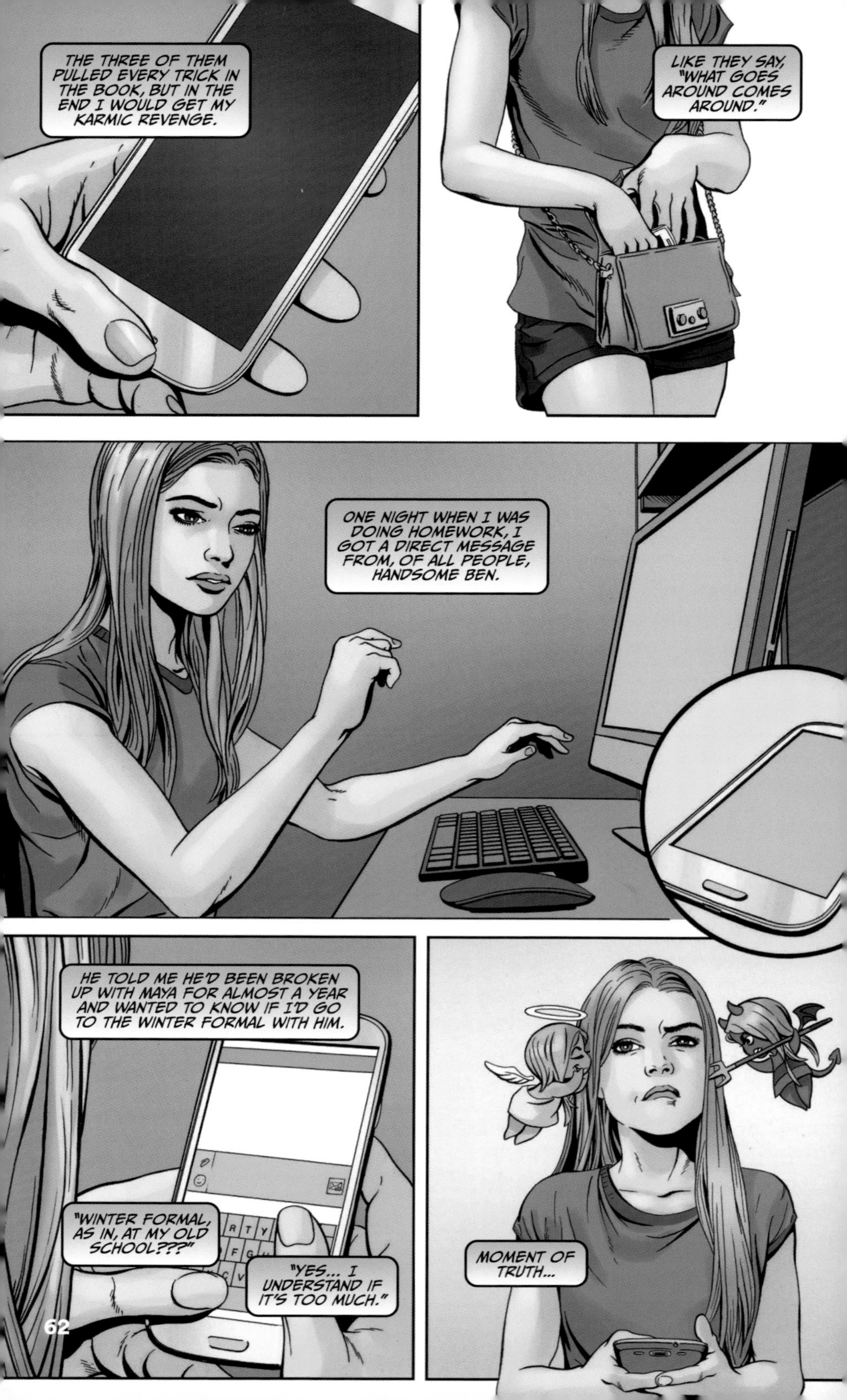
THE THREE OF THEM PULLED EVERY TRICK IN THE BOOK, BUT IN THE END I WOULD GET MY KARMIC REVENGE.
LIKE THEY SAY, "WHAT GOES AROUND COMES AROUND."
ONE NIGHT WHEN I WAS DOING HOMEWORK, I GOT A DIRECT MESSAGE FROM, OF ALL PEOPLE, HANDSOME BEN.
HE TOLD ME HE'D BEEN BROKEN UP WITH MAYA FOR ALMOST A YEAR AND WANTED TO KNOW IF I'D GO TO THE WINTER FORMAL WITH HIM.
"WINTER FORMAL, AS IN, AT MY OLD SCHOOL???"
"YES... I UNDERSTAND IF IT'S TOO MUCH."
MOMENT OF TRUTH...

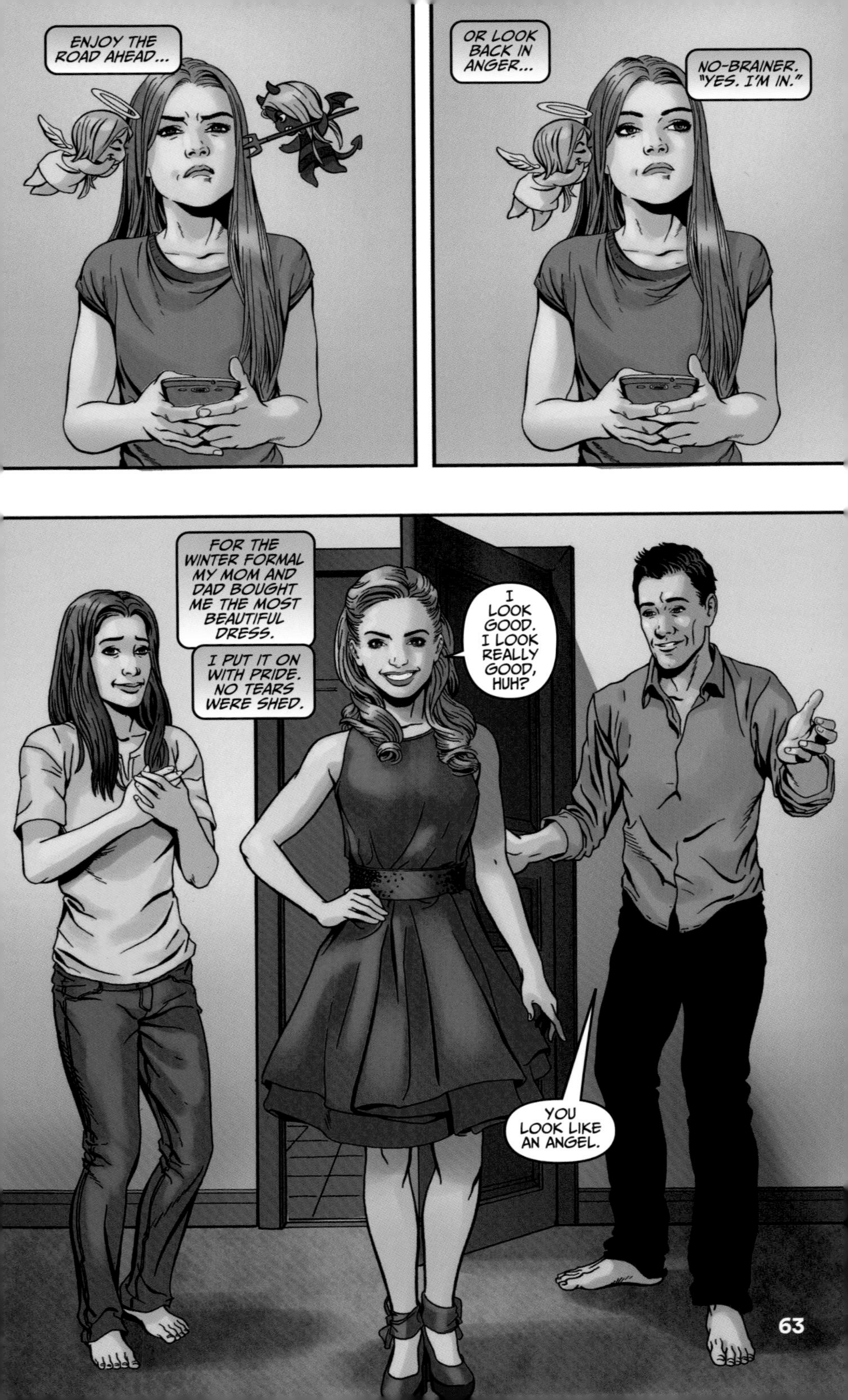
ENJOY THE ROAD AHEAD...
OR LOOK BACK IN ANGER...
NO-BRAINER. "YES. I'M IN."
FOR THE WINTER FORMAL MY MOM AND DAD BOUGHT ME THE MOST BEAUTIFUL DRESS.
I PUT IT ON WITH PRIDE. NO TEARS WERE SHED.
I LOOK GOOD. I LOOK REALLY GOOD, HUH?
YOU LOOK LIKE AN ANGEL.

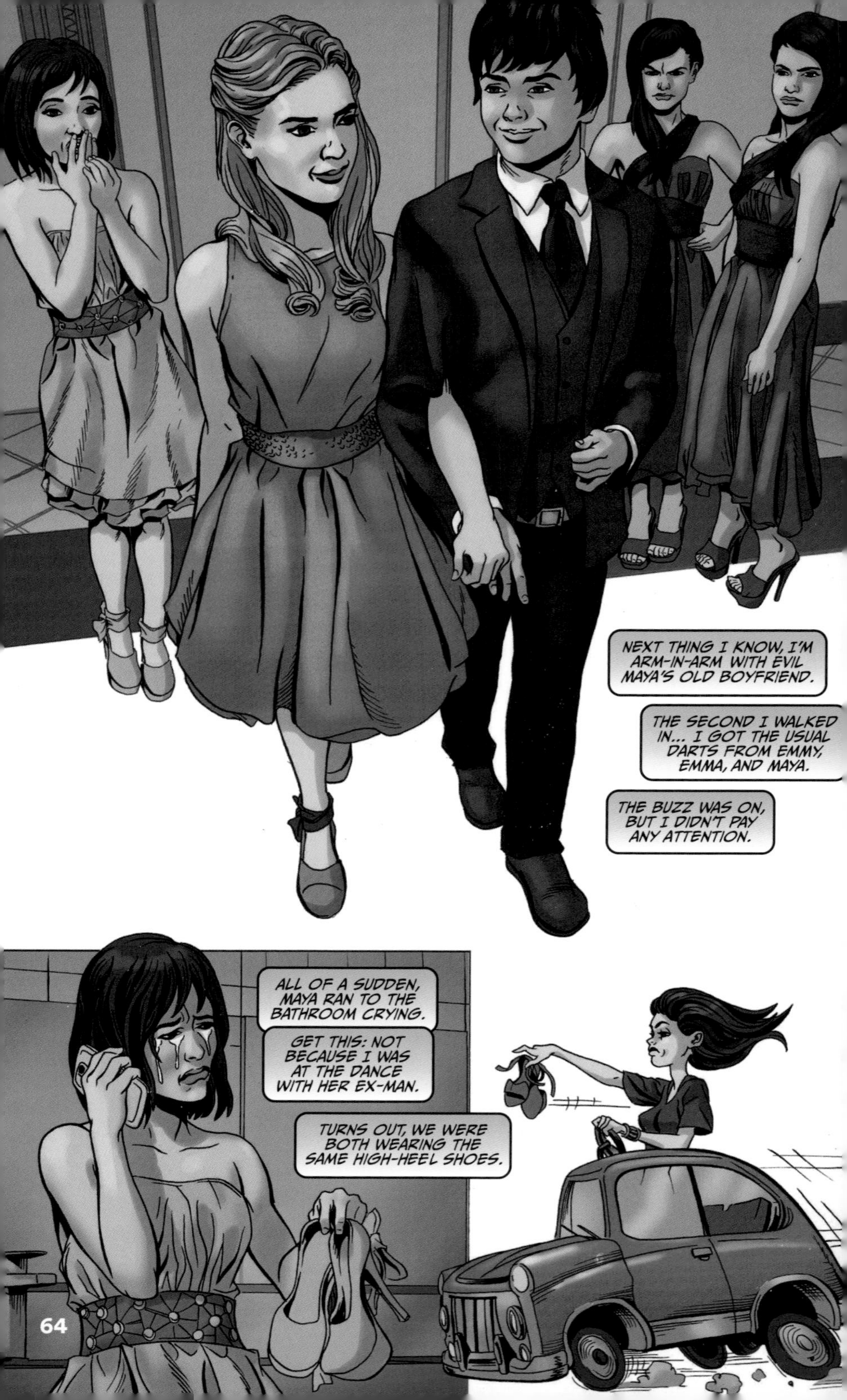
NEXT THING I KNOW, I'M ARM-IN-ARM WITH EVIL MAYA'S OLD BOYFRIEND.
THE SECOND I WALKED IN... I GOT THE USUAL DARTS FROM EMMY, EMMA, AND MAYA.
THE BUZZ WAS ON, BUT I DIDN'T PAY ANY ATTENTION.
ALL OF A SUDDEN, MAYA RAN TO THE BATHROOM CRYING.
GET THIS: NOT BECAUSE I WAS AT THE DANCE WITH HER EX-MAN.
TURNS OUT, WE WERE BOTH WEARING THE SAME HIGH-HEEL SHOES.

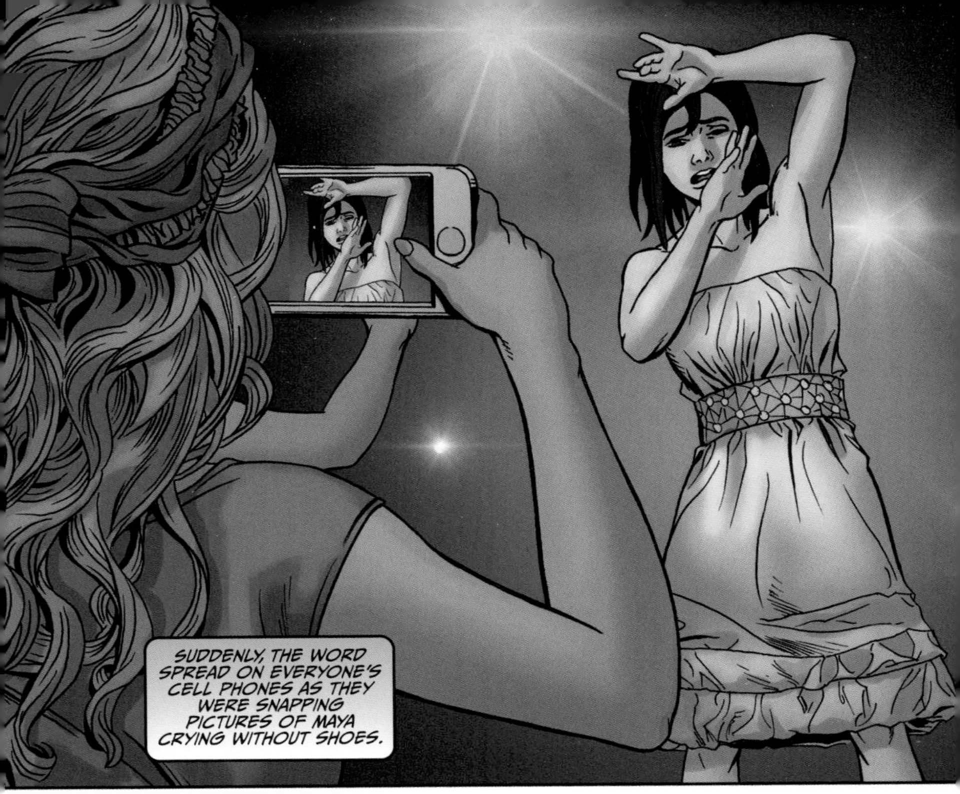
SUDDENLY, THE WORD SPREAD ON EVERYONE'S CELL PHONES AS THEY WERE SNAPPING PICTURES OF MAYA CRYING WITHOUT SHOES.

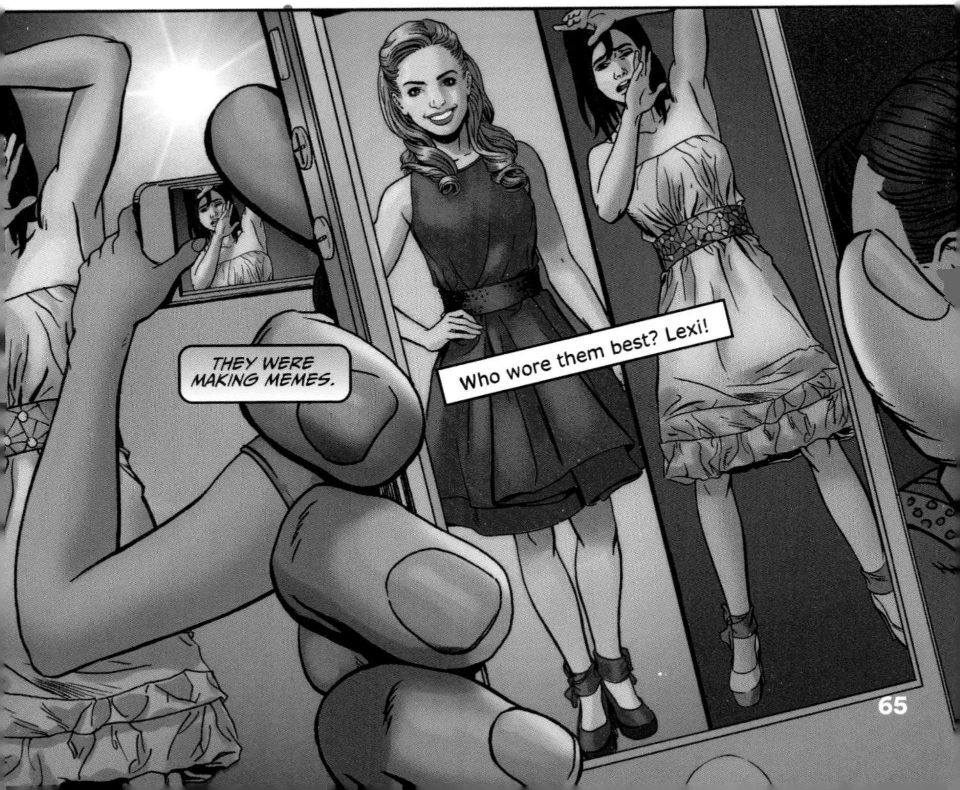
THEY WERE MAKING MEMES.
Who wore them best? Lexi!

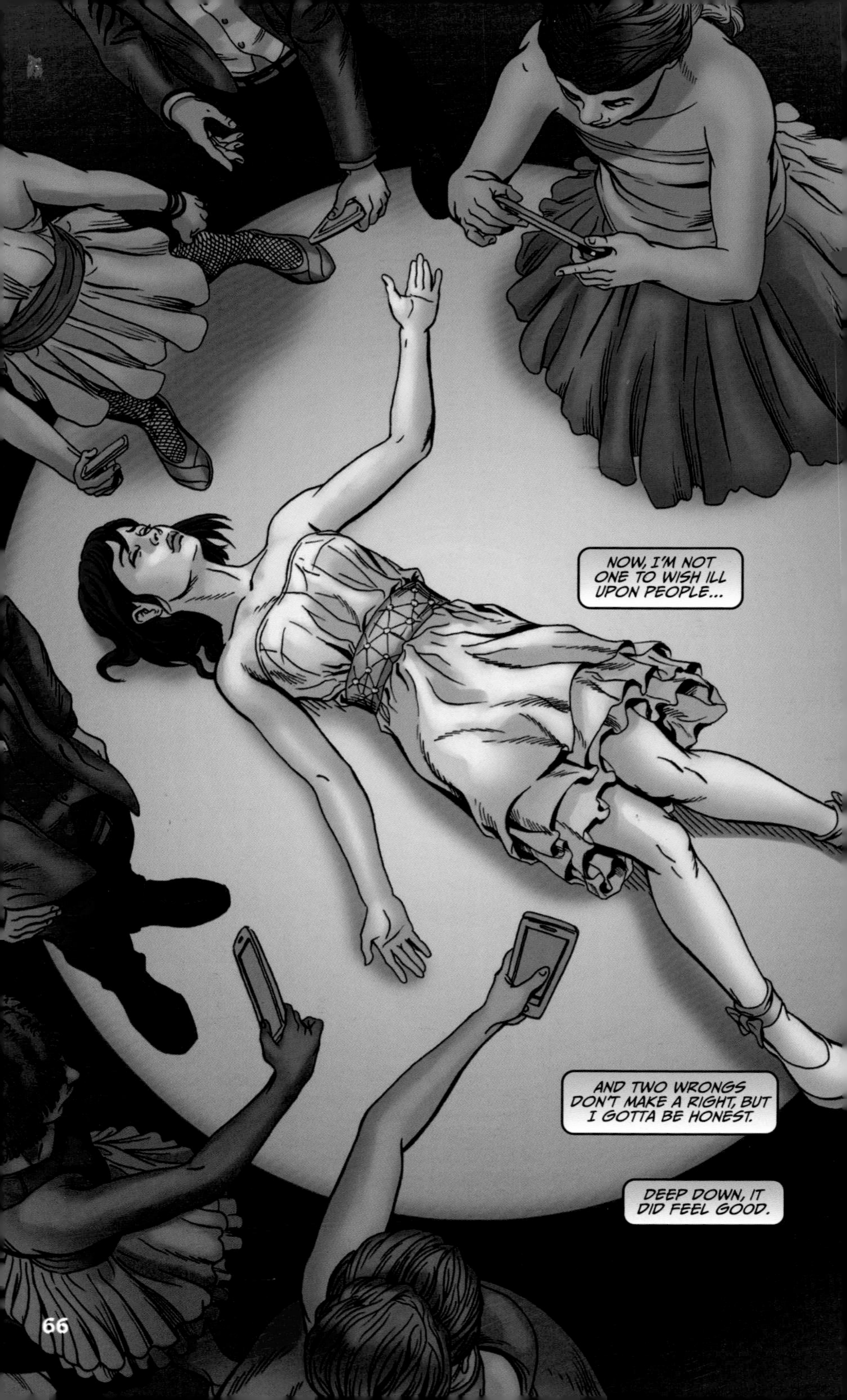
NOW, I'M NOT ONE TO WISH ILL UPON PEOPLE...
AND TWO WRONGS DON'T MAKE A RIGHT, BUT I GOTTA BE HONEST.
DEEP DOWN, IT DID FEEL GOOD.

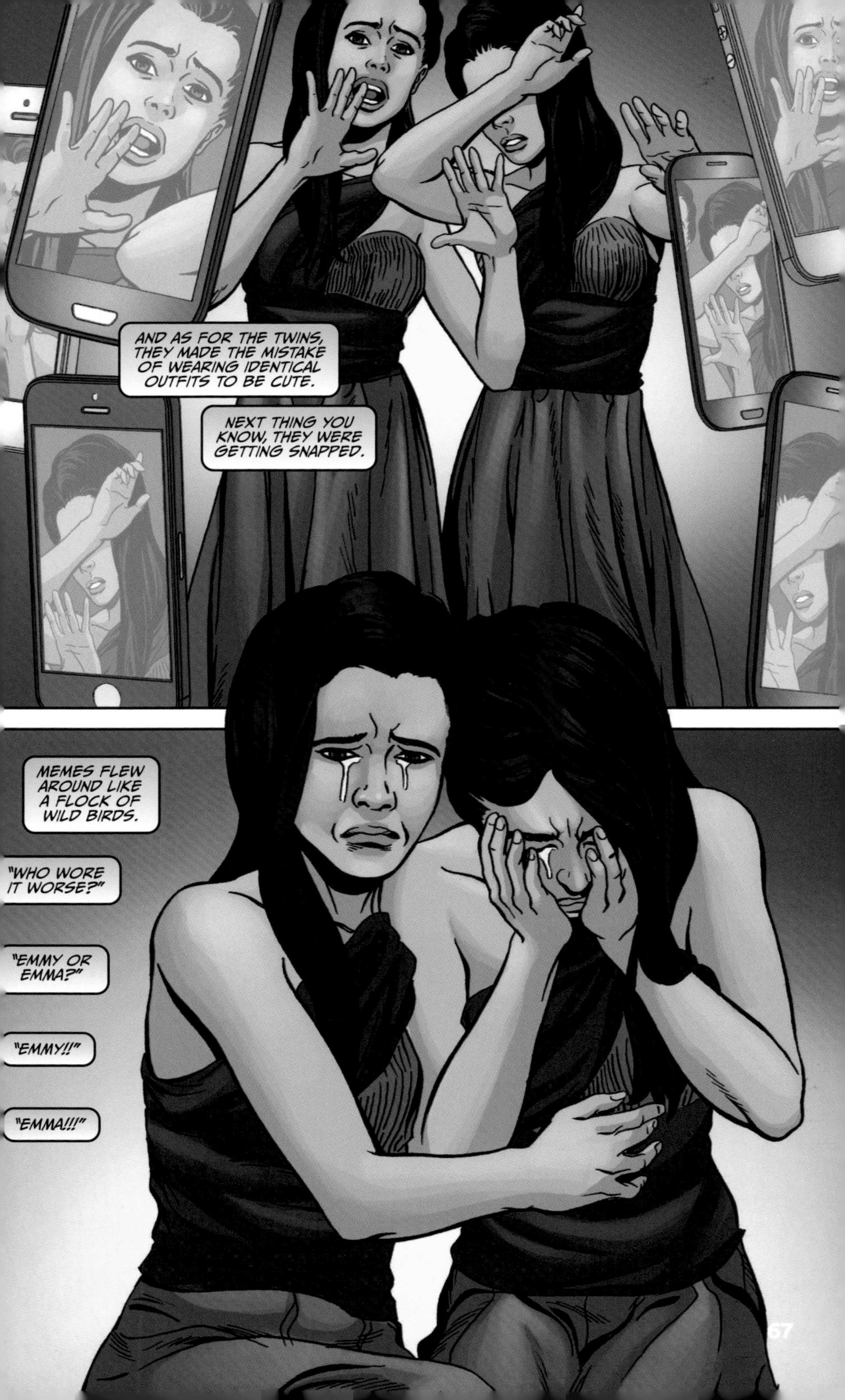
AND AS FOR THE TWINS, THEY MADE THE MISTAKE OF WEARING IDENTICAL OUTFITS TO BE CUTE.
NEXT THING YOU KNOW, THEY WERE GETTING SNAPPED.
MEMES FLEW AROUND LIKE A FLOCK OF WILD BIRDS.
"WHO WORE IT WORSE?"
"EMMY OR EMMA?"
"EMMY!!"
"EMMA!!!"

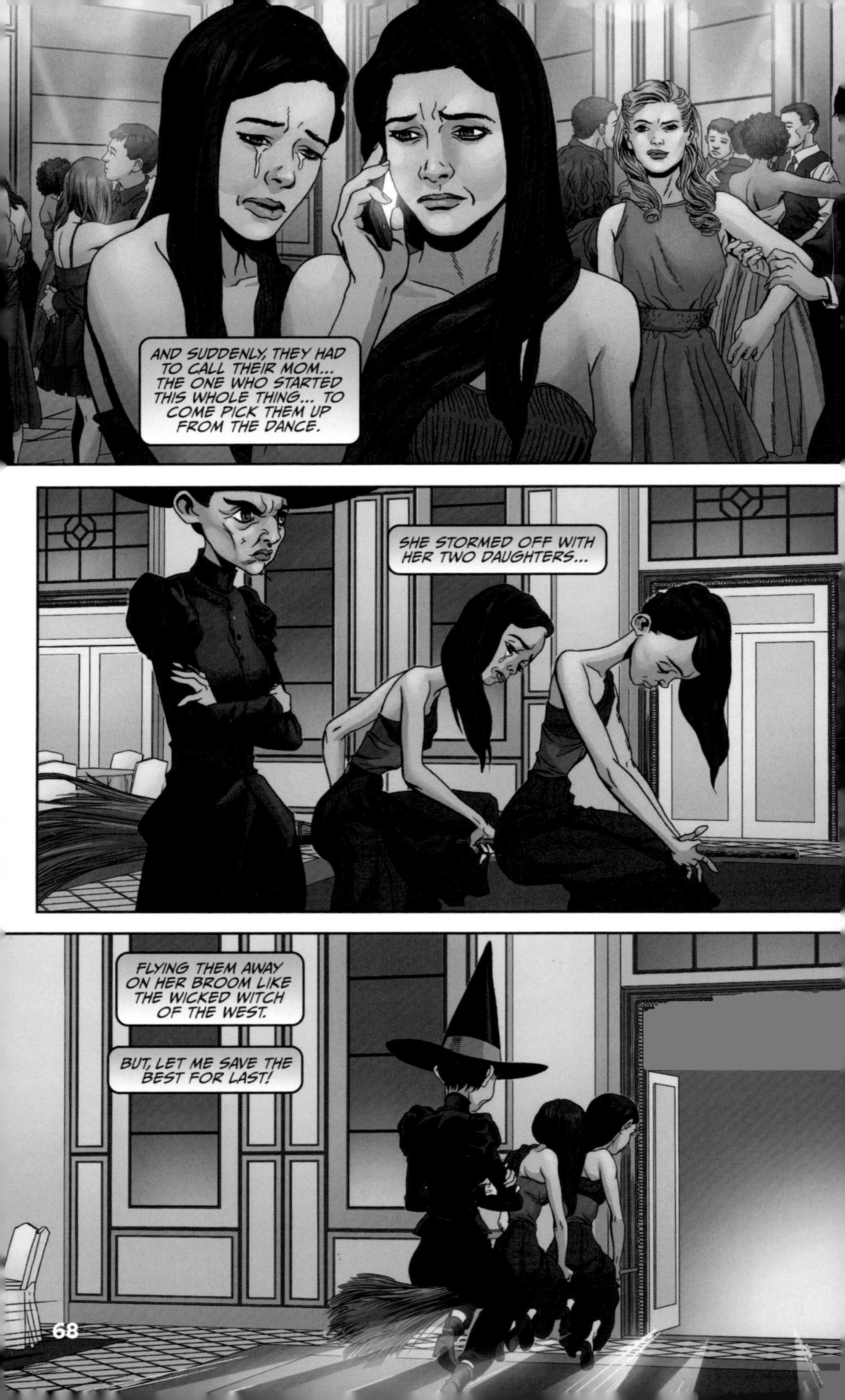
AND SUDDENLY, THEY HAD TO CALL THEIR MOM... THE ONE WHO STARTED THIS WHOLE THING... TO COME PICK THEM UP FROM THE DANCE.
SHE STORMED OFF WITH HER TWO DAUGHTERS...
FLYING THEM AWAY ON HER BROOM LIKE THE WICKED WITCH OF THE WEST.
BUT, LET ME SAVE THE BEST FOR LAST!

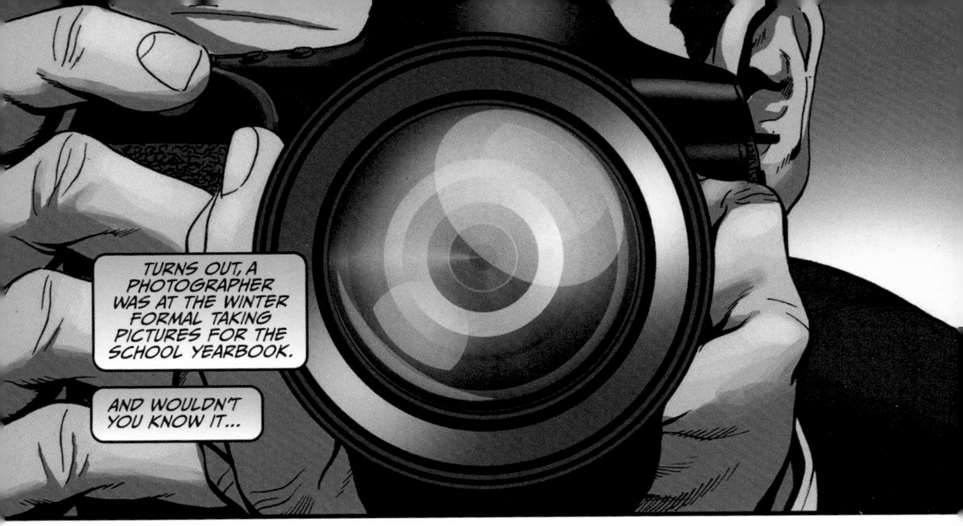
TURNS OUT, A PHOTOGRAPHER WAS AT THE WINTER FORMAL TAKING PICTURES FOR THE SCHOOL YEARBOOK.
AND WOULDN'T YOU KNOW IT...

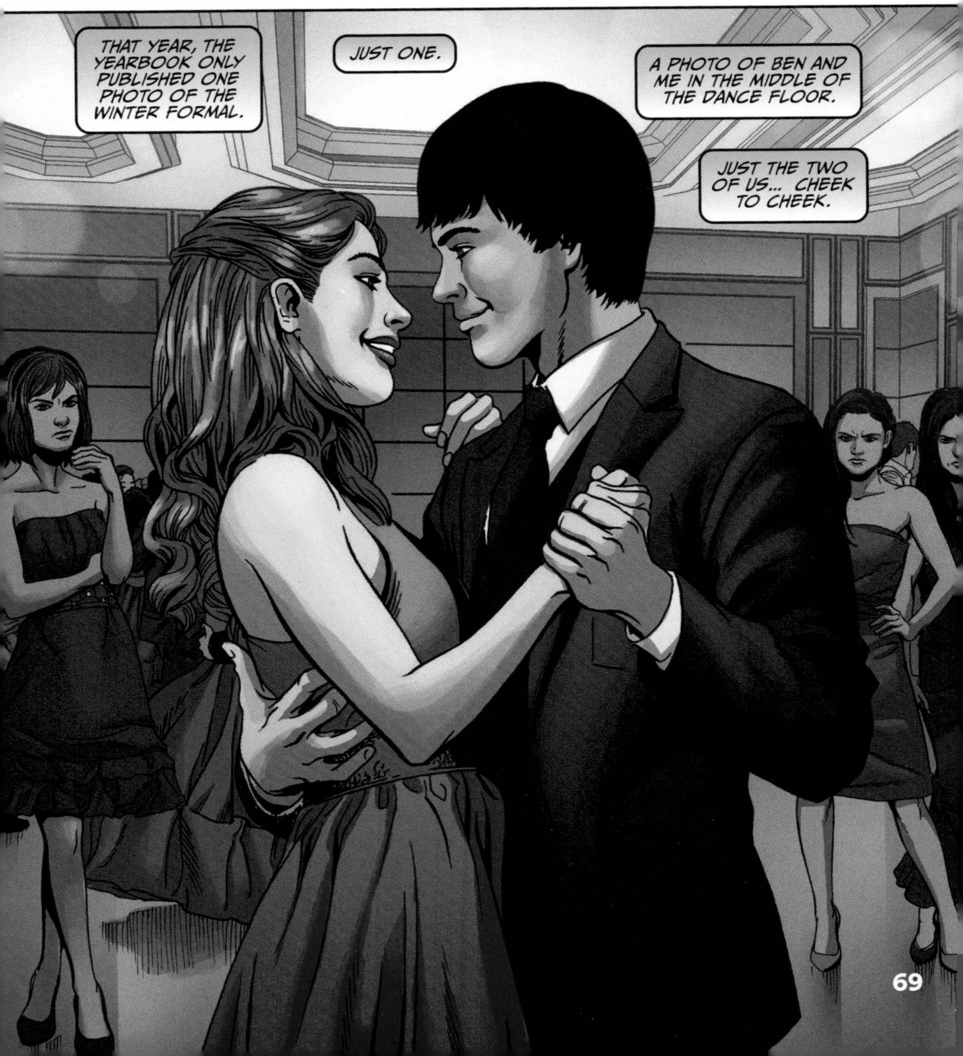
THAT YEAR, THE YEARBOOK ONLY PUBLISHED ONE PHOTO OF THE WINTER FORMAL.
JUST ONE.
A PHOTO OF BEN AND ME IN THE MIDDLE OF THE DANCE FLOOR.
JUST THE TWO OF US... CHEEK TO CHEEK.

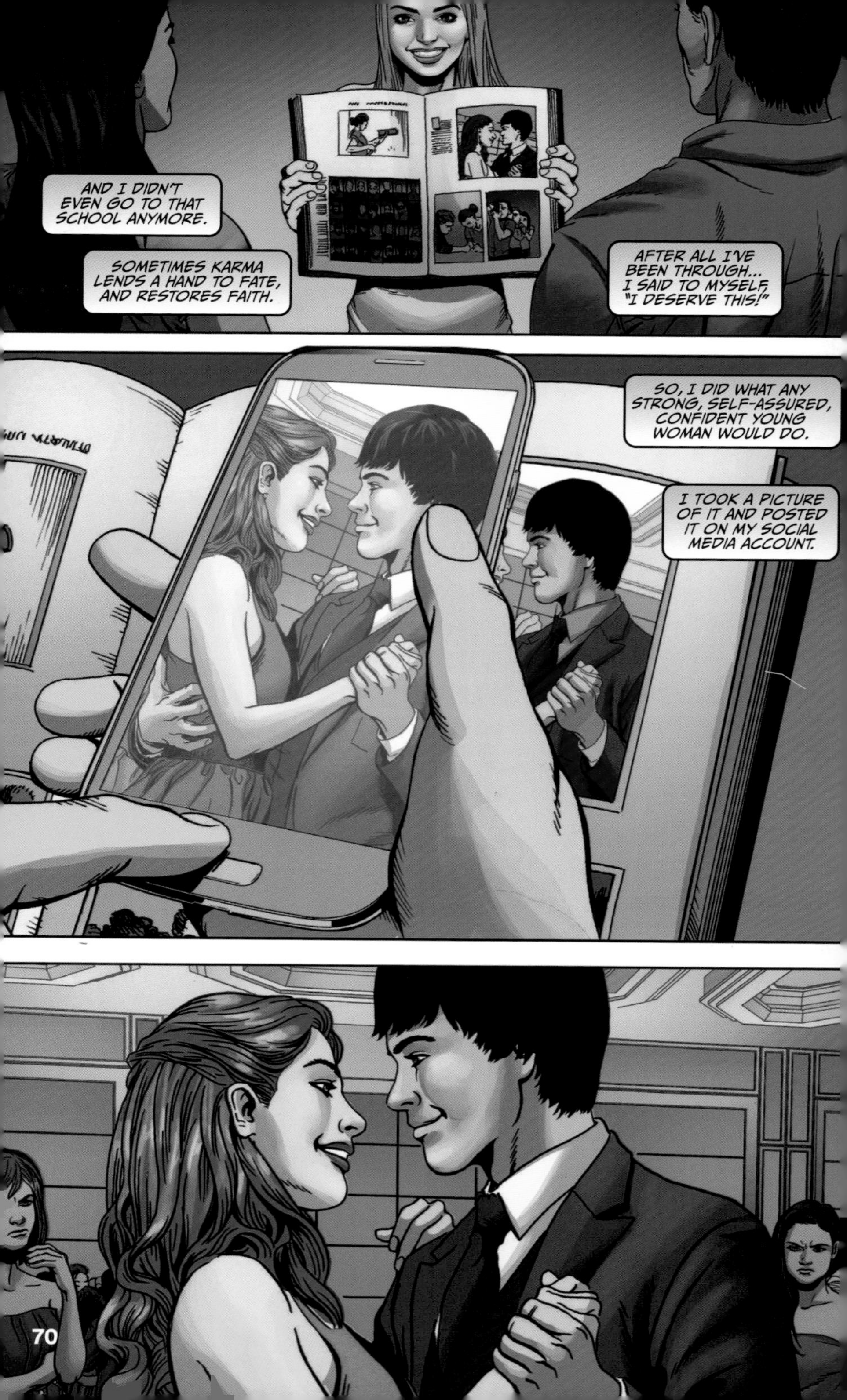
AND I DIDN'T EVEN GO TO THAT SCHOOL ANYMORE.
SOMETIMES KARMA LENDS A HAND TO FATE, AND RESTORES FAITH.
AFTER ALL I'VE BEEN THROUGH... I SAID TO MYSELF, "I DESERVE THIS!"
SO, I DID WHAT ANY STRONG, SELF-ASSURED, CONFIDENT YOUNG WOMAN WOULD DO.
I TOOK A PICTURE OF IT AND POSTED IT ON MY SOCIAL MEDIA ACCOUNT.

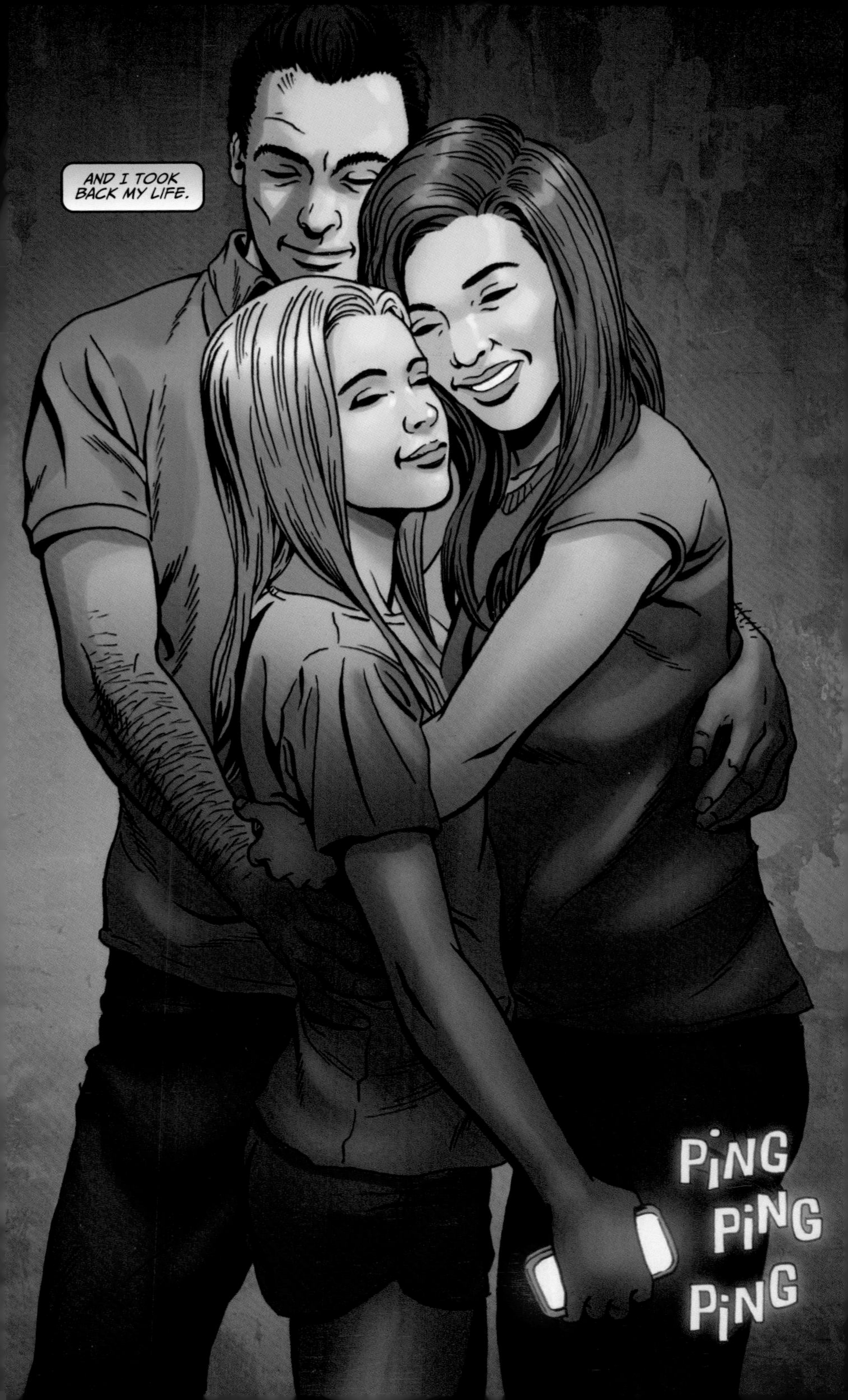
AND I TOOK BACK MY LIFE.
PING PING PING

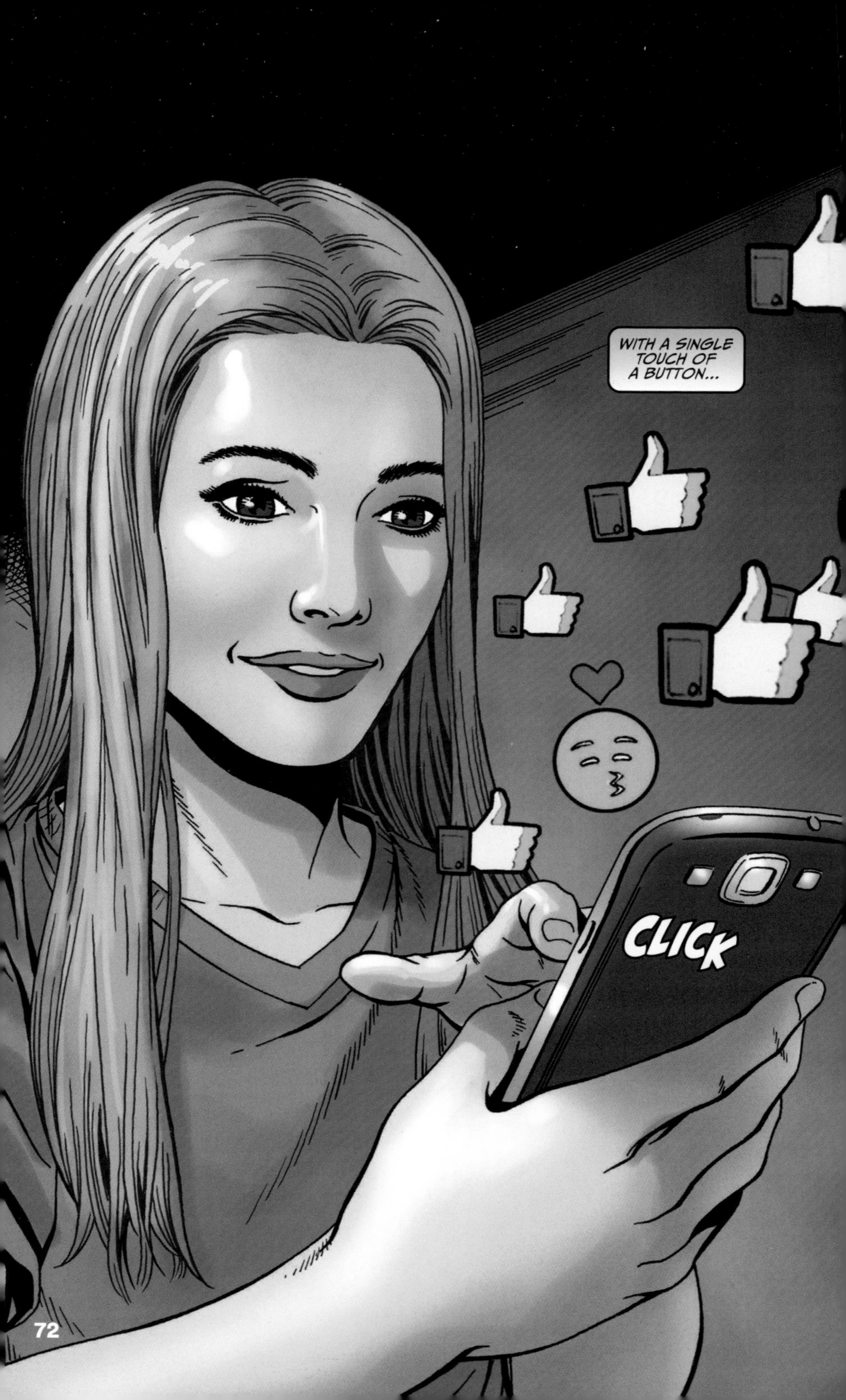
WITH A SINGLE TOUCH OF A BUTTON...
CLICK

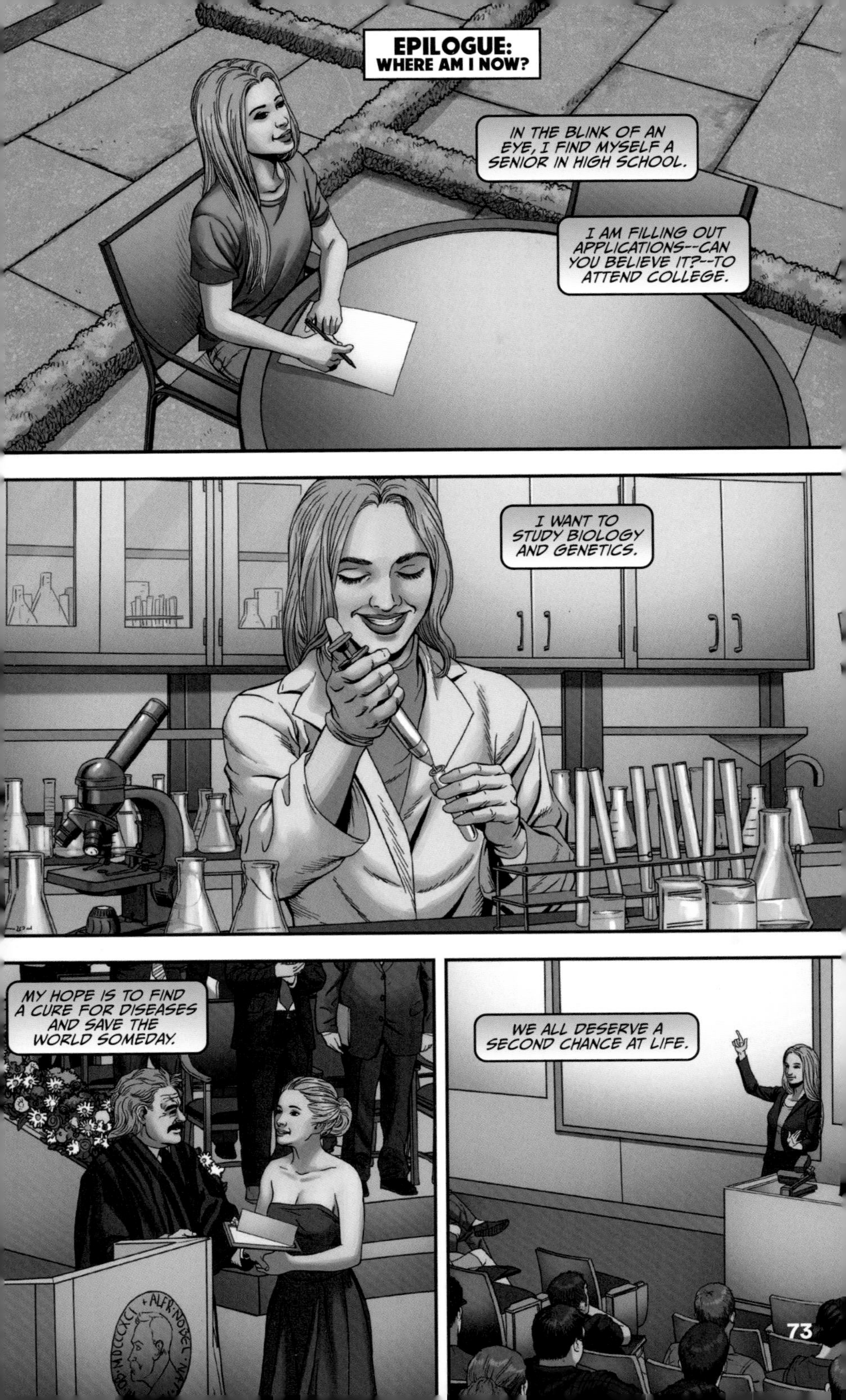
EPILOGUE: WHERE AM I NOW?
IN THE BLINK OF AN EYE, I FIND MYSELF A SENIOR IN HIGH SCHOOL.
I AM FILLING OUT APPLICATIONS--CAN YOU BELIEVE IT?--TO ATTEND COLLEGE.
I WANT TO STUDY BIOLOGY AND GENETICS.
MY HOPE IS TO FIND A CURE FOR DISEASES AND SAVE THE WORLD SOMEDAY.
WE ALL DESERVE A SECOND CHANCE AT LIFE.

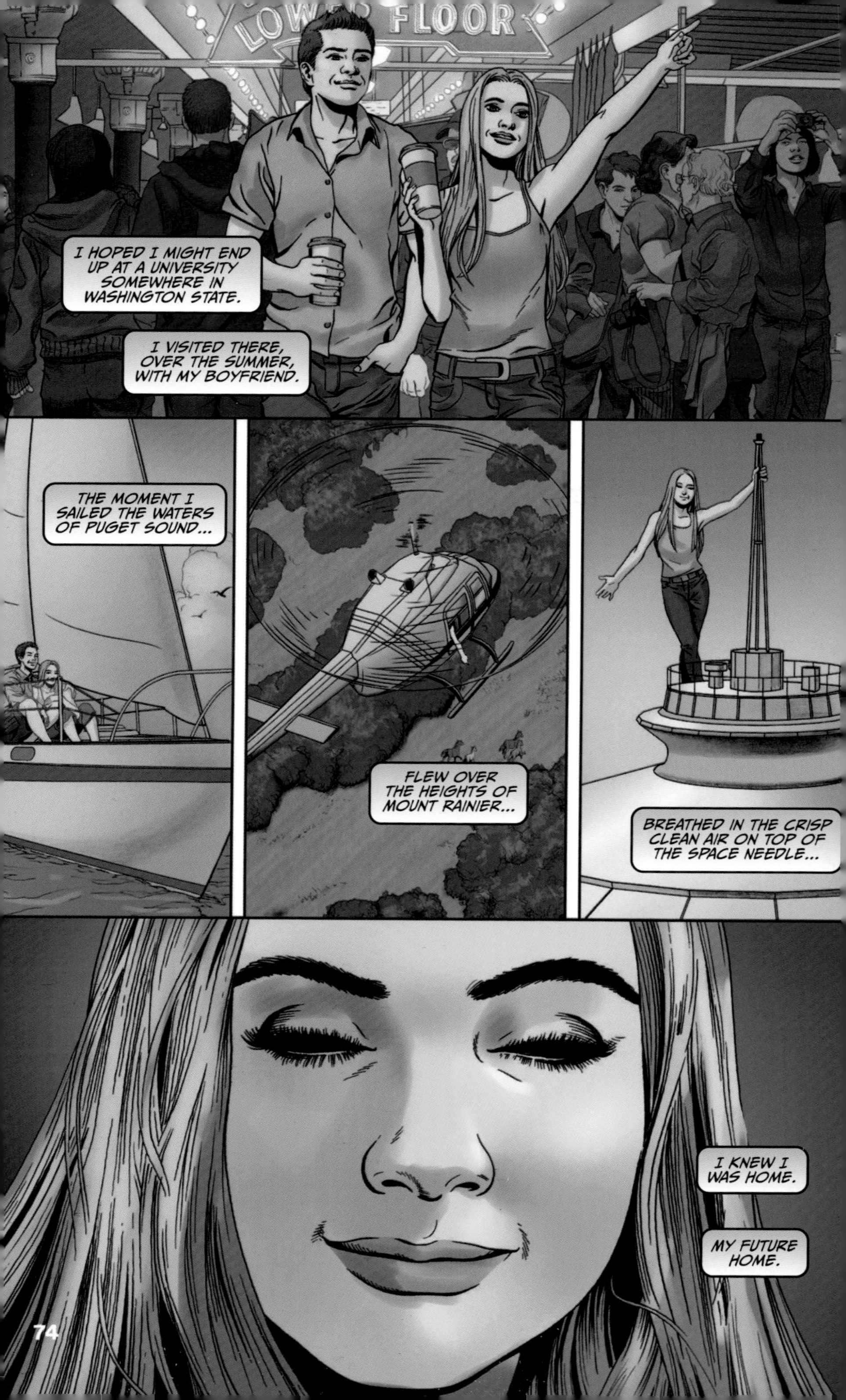
LOWER FLOOR
I HOPED I MIGHT END UP AT A UNIVERSITY SOMEWHERE IN WASHINGTON STATE.
I VISITED THERE, OVER THE SUMMER, WITH MY BOYFRIEND.
THE MOMENT I SAILED THE WATERS OF PUGET SOUND...
FLEW OVER THE HEIGHTS OF MOUNT RAINIER...
BREATHED IN THE CRISP CLEAN AIR ON TOP OF THE SPACE NEEDLE...
I KNEW I WAS HOME.
MY FUTURE HOME.

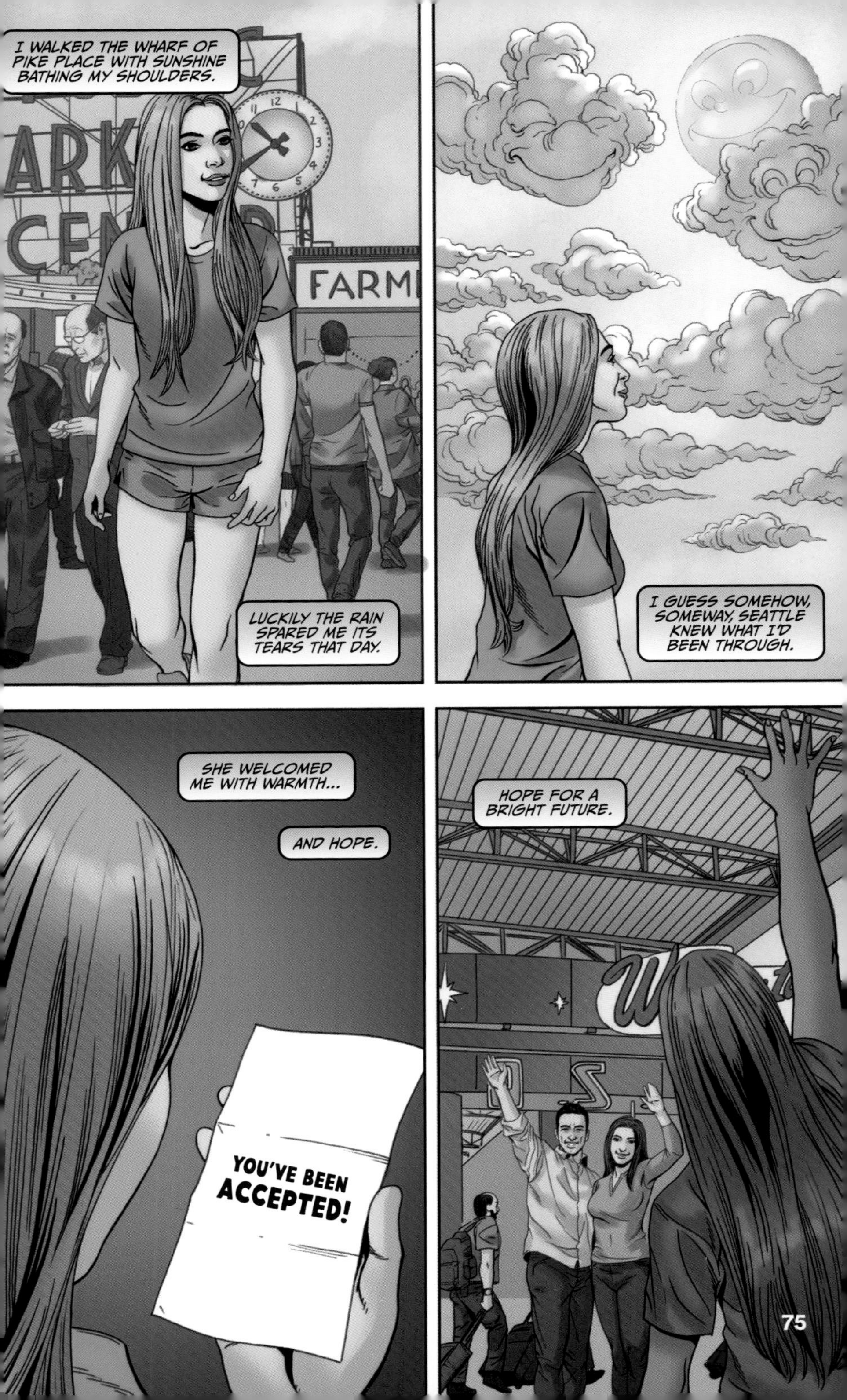
I WALKED THE WHARF OF PIKE PLACE WITH SUNSHINE BATHING MY SHOULDERS.
FARM
LUCKILY THE RAIN SPARED ME ITS TEARS THAT DAY.
I GUESS SOMEHOW, SOMEWAY, SEATTLE KNEW WHAT I'D BEEN THROUGH.
SHE WELCOMED ME WITH WARMTH...
AND HOPE.
YOU'VE BEEN ACCEPTED!
HOPE FOR A BRIGHT FUTURE.

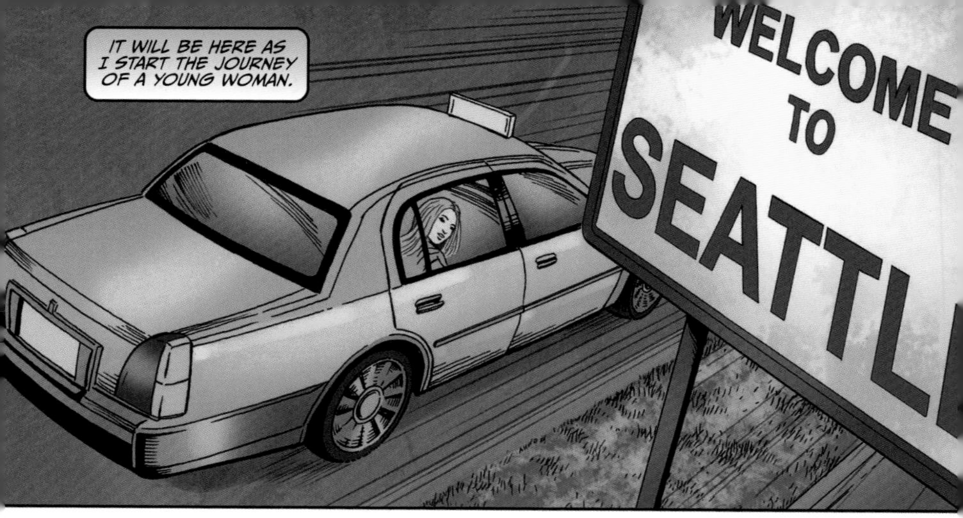
IT WILL BE HERE AS I START THE JOURNEY OF A YOUNG WOMAN.
WELCOME TO SEATTL

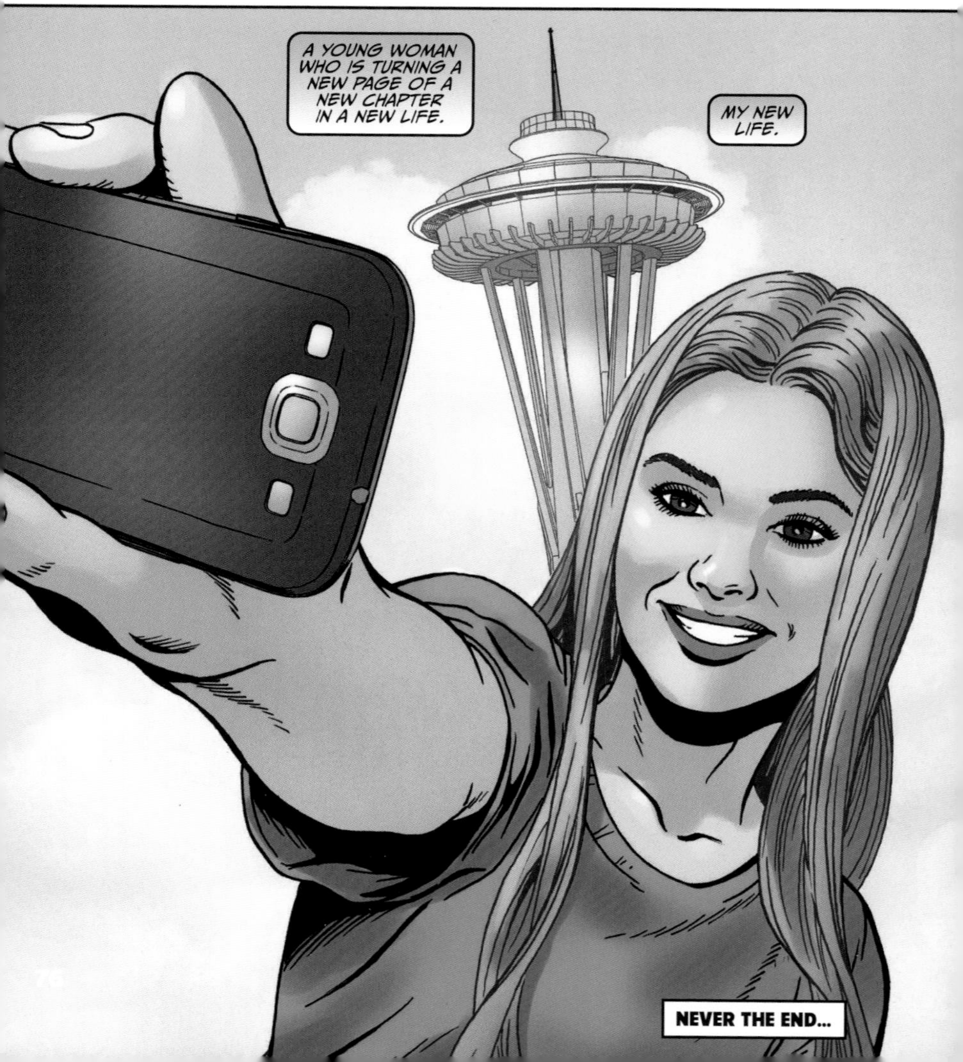
A YOUNG WOMAN WHO IS TURNING A NEW PAGE OF A NEW CHAPTER IN A NEW LIFE.
MY NEW LIFE.
NEVER THE END...

ABOUT OUR AUTHOR

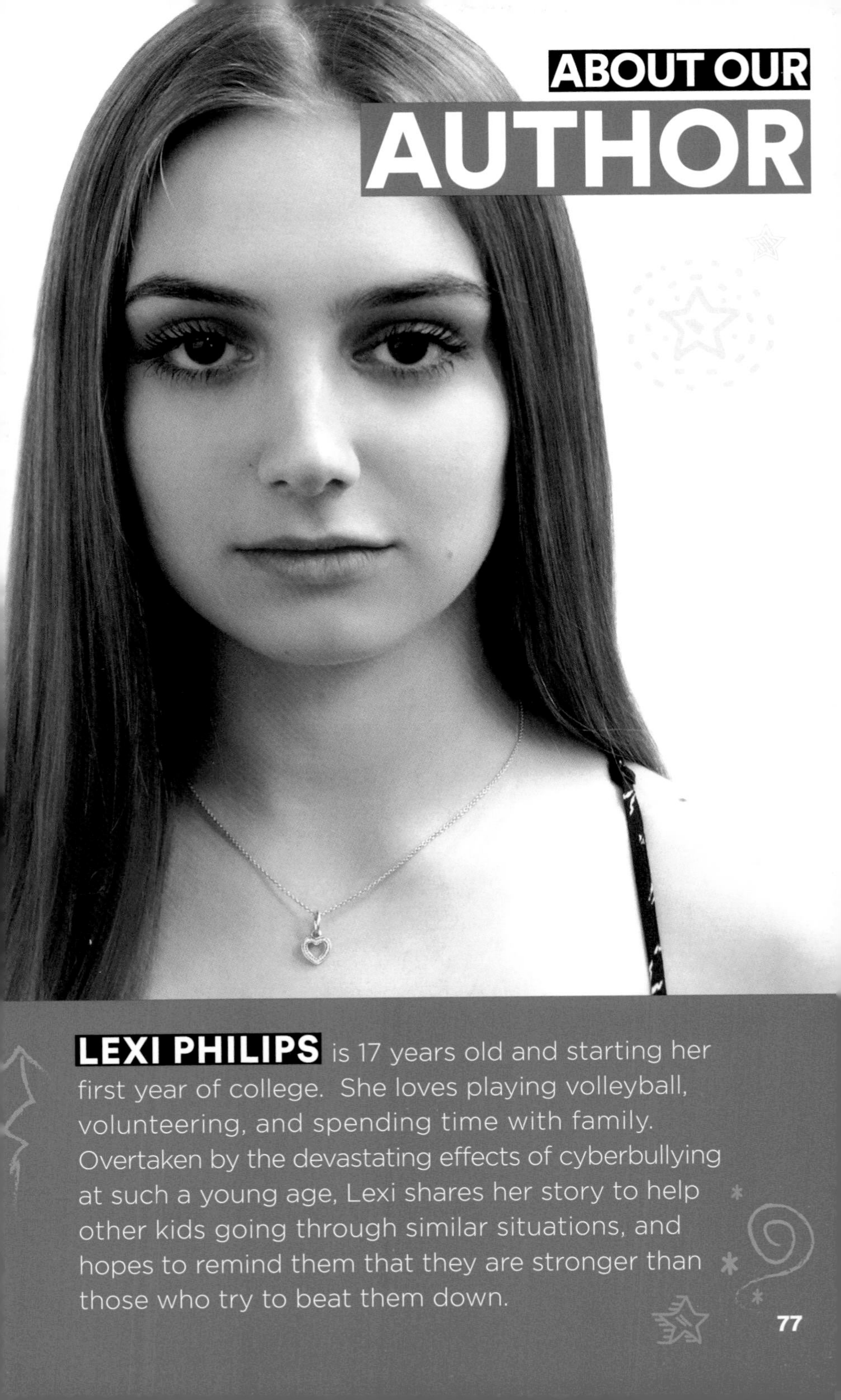

LEXI PHILIPS is 17 years old and starting her first year of college. She loves playing volleyball, volunteering, and spending time with family. Overtaken by the devastating effects of cyberbullying at such a young age, Lexi shares her story to help other kids going through similar situations, and hopes to remind them that they are stronger than those who try to beat them down.

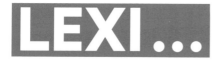

LEXI...

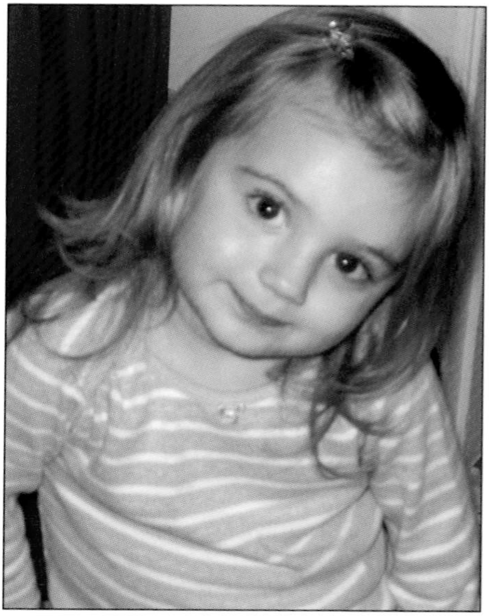

When I was little, I used to make this face when I wanted something (I'm not very proud of this now!).

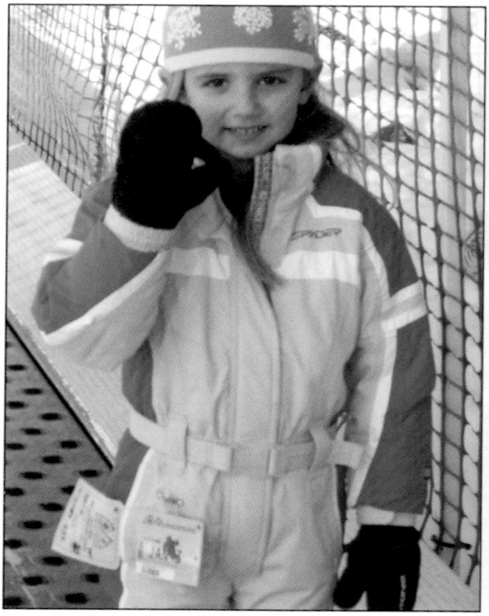

When I was about 7 years old, I found my first passion ... skiing!

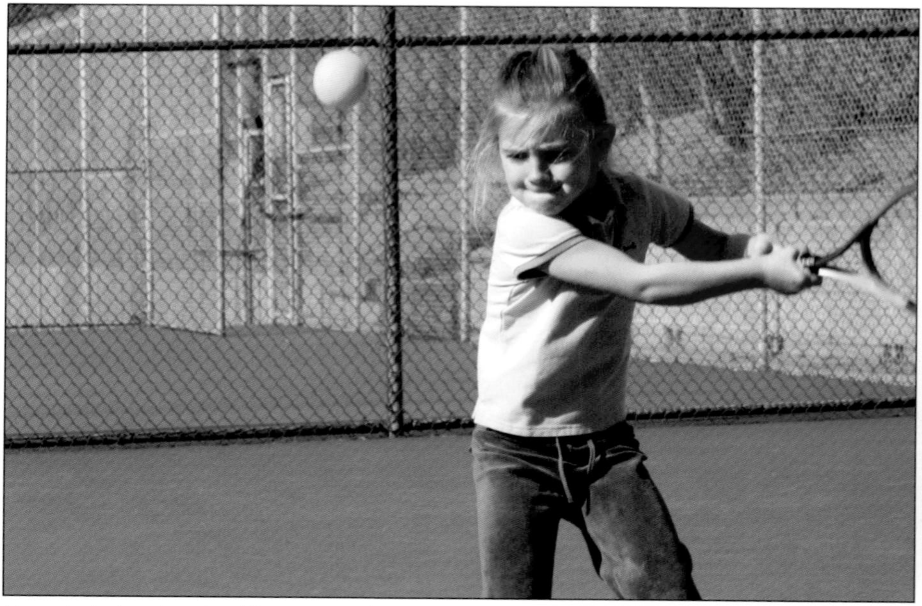

I loved playing tennis with my grandpa every weekend!

...LEXI

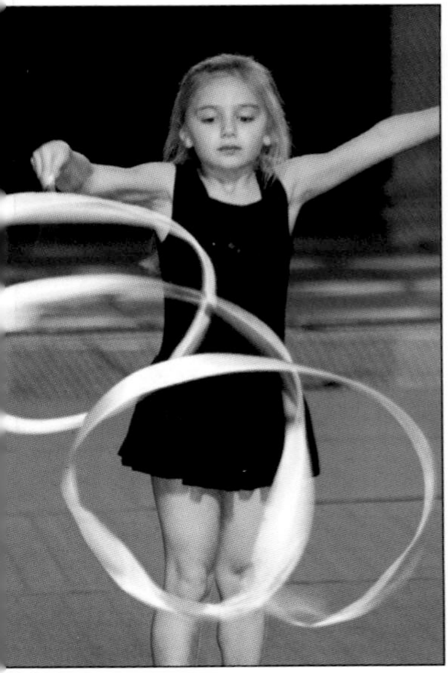

Gymnastics was my favorite thing to do with my friends!

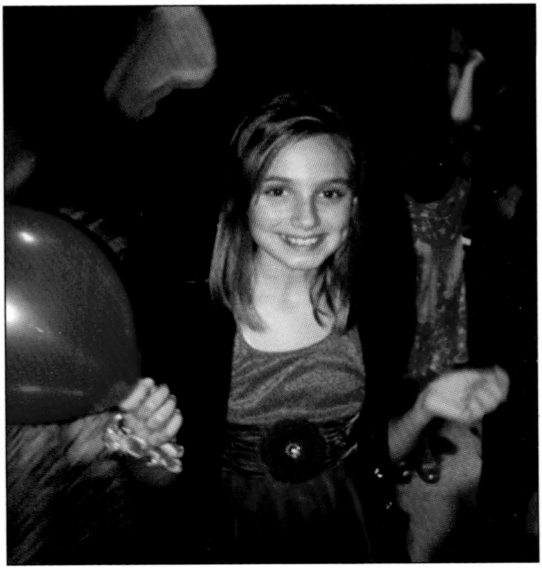

Going out to dances helped me forget about my cyberbullies!

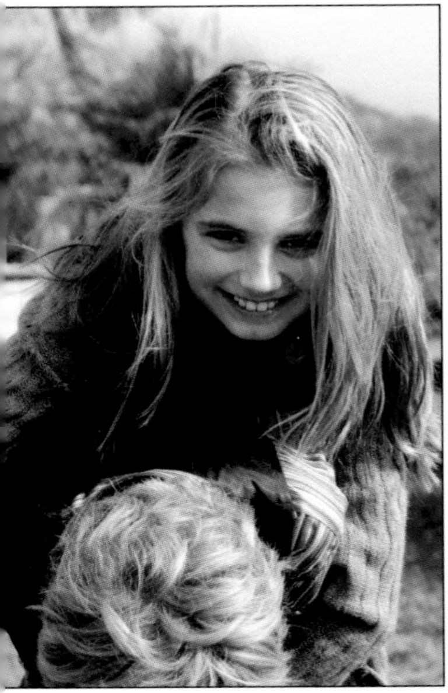

My little brother and I used to mess with each other all the time!

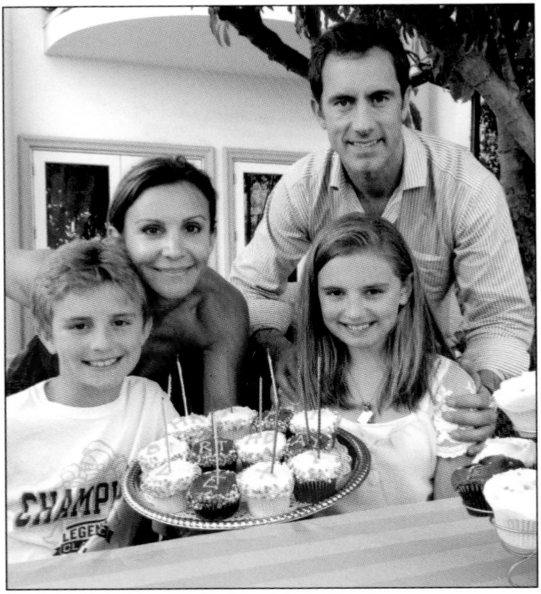

My mom, dad, and brother loved me no matter what, and helped me through everything.

LEXI...

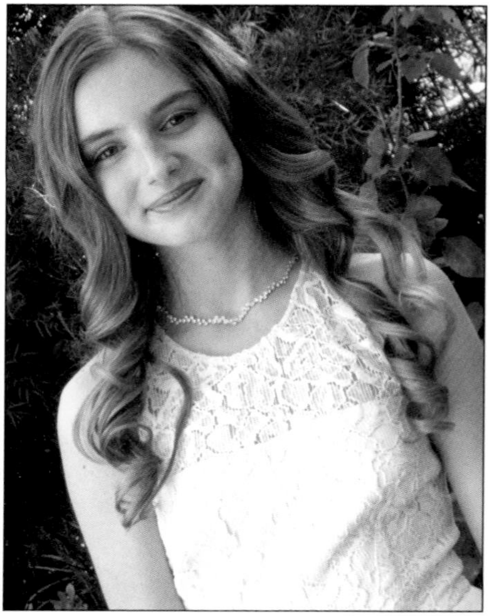

Soon, I made it through middle school! This is me on 8th grade graduation day!

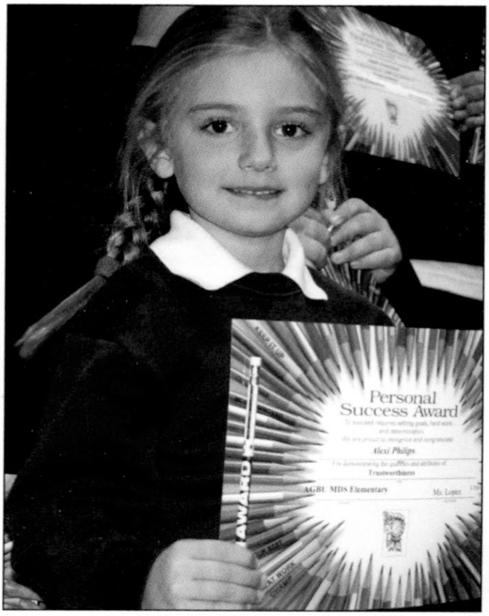
Personal
Success Award
Alexi Philips
AGBU MDS Elementary
Ms. Lopez
AWARD

When I was in first grade, I got an award for trustworthiness!

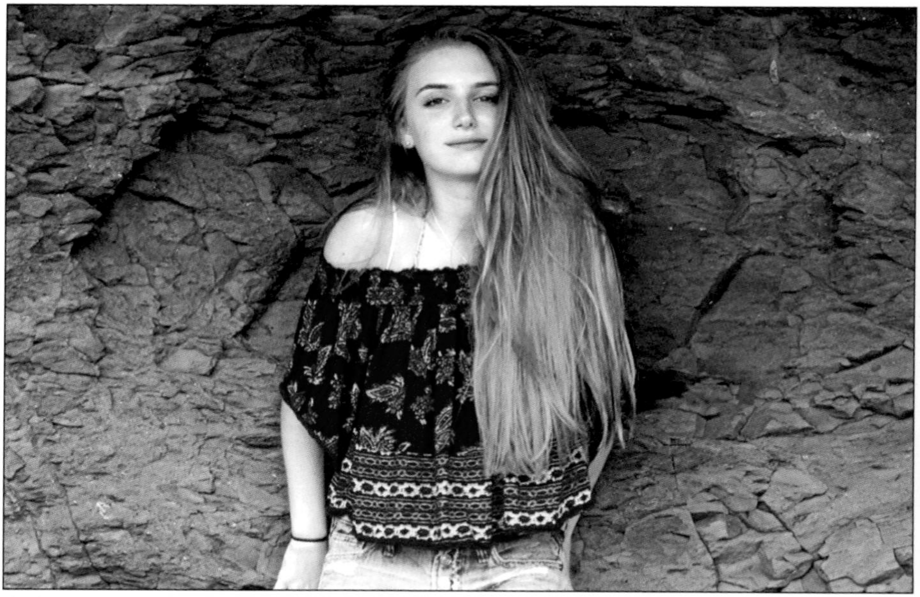

Today, I am the happiest I've ever been, surrounded by all the people that I love!

TAKE 5!

FIVE PARENT TAKE-AWAYS ABOUT CYBERBULLYING

MARY AIKEN, PhD

is a cyberpsychologist. Mary specializes in the impact of technology on human behavior, and has written extensively on issues relating to the intersection between humankind and technology – or as she describes it "where humans and technology collide."

CYBERBULLYING IS THE "NEW BULLYING."

Parents and students need to be aware that bullying has progressed into the technological era. Bullying used to be something that occurred on school grounds. Today, cyberbullies can attack your child 24/7 in the privacy of your own home.

TELL A TRUSTED ADULT IF CYBERBULLYING OCCURS.

More often times than not, the victim of cyberbullying doesn't report it. Save the evidence of the bullying, print it out, and show it to a parent, a principal, or counselor at school. Whatever you do, don't retaliate. The electronic evidence of abuse will be helpful if law enforcement has to get involved.

PARENTS SHOULD MONITOR ALL SOCIAL MEDIA ACCOUNTS.

Most parents have no idea what social media accounts, smart phone apps, or online groups their kids belong to. For the safety of your children, it's vital that parents know what apps their children are using with passcodes. Respecting their privacy is important, but their safety from online predators, cyberbullies, and "frenemies" (friend enemies) is paramount.

DISCONNECT MORE THAN YOU CONNECT.

Sure, the world today is much different than when our parents were growing up. However, social media, texting, emailing, and group chat should take a backseat to good, old-fashioned, in-person communication. Believe it or not, life can be meaningful when it's just human-to-human. Try to connect more in person than on a device.

ONCE YOU POST IT, IT'S FOR LIFE.

Many young people make the mistake of posting pictures of themselves for attention. Don't! One thing about the Internet, there is no "escape" button. Pause before you post. Once it's out there in cyberspace, you can be re-offended over and over again. Practice proper network hygiene at all times.

THE STORY DOESN'T END HERE...

Why did you agree to do a book about cyberbullying?

VISIT
ZUIKERPRESS.COM

To learn more about Lexi's story, see behind-the-scenes videos of Lexi and her family, and learn more about how to cope with **CYBERBULLYING** .

Our **WEBSITE** is another resource to help our readers deal with the issues that they face every day. Log on to find advice from experts, links to helpful organizations and literature, and more real-life experiences from young people just like you.

Spotlighting young writers with heartfelt stories that enlighten and inspire.

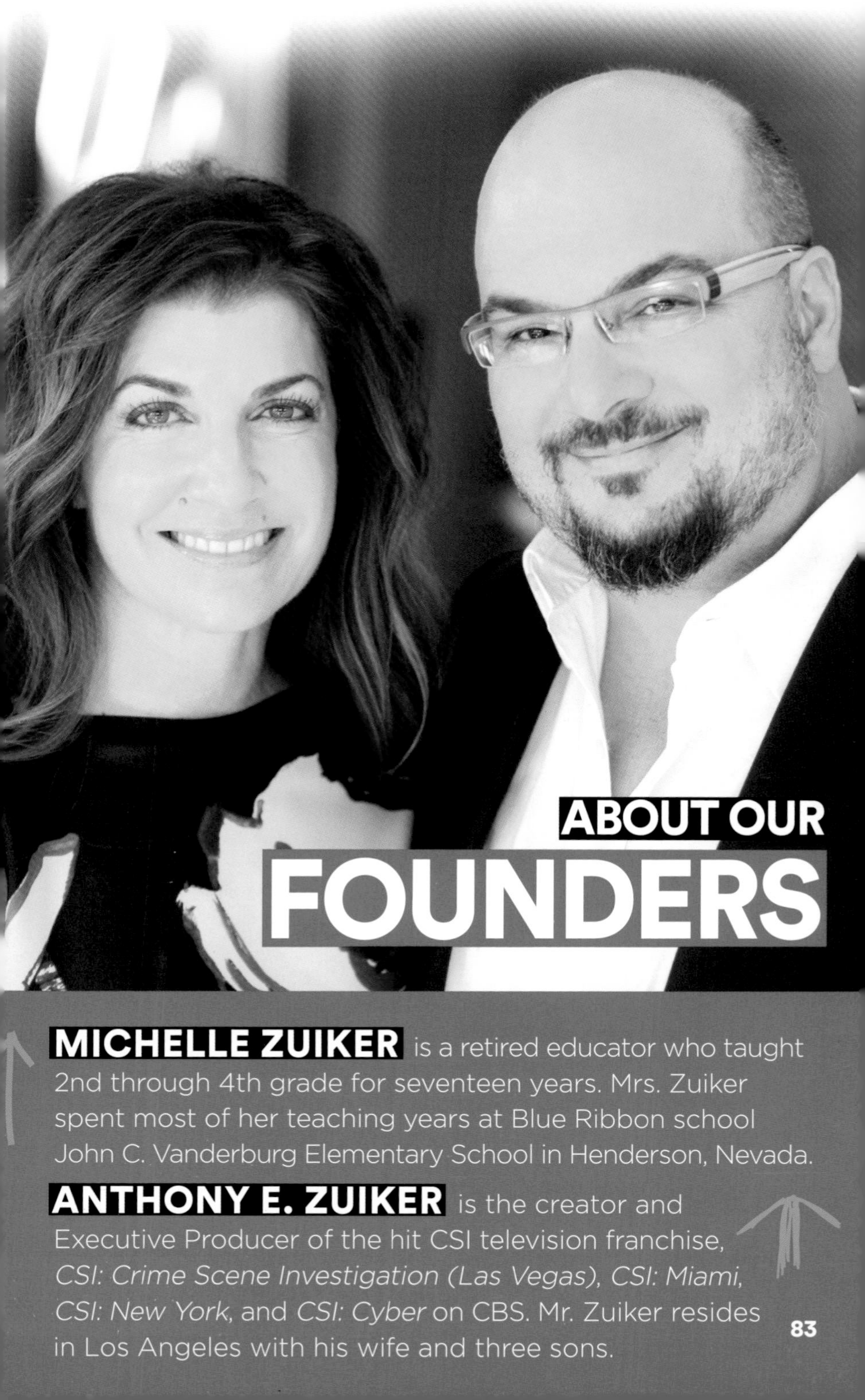

ABOUT OUR FOUNDERS

MICHELLE ZUIKER is a retired educator who taught 2nd through 4th grade for seventeen years. Mrs. Zuiker spent most of her teaching years at Blue Ribbon school John C. Vanderburg Elementary School in Henderson, Nevada.

ANTHONY E. ZUIKER is the creator and Executive Producer of the hit CSI television franchise, *CSI: Crime Scene Investigation (Las Vegas)*, *CSI: Miami*, *CSI: New York*, and *CSI: Cyber* on CBS. Mr. Zuiker resides in Los Angeles with his wife and three sons.

ABOUT OUR
ILLUSTRATORS
& EDITOR...

NAM KIM—PENCILER

is a Philadelphia-based artist, founder and director of Studio Imaginary Lines, an all-purpose design house which produces original content for comic books, video games, mobile apps and commercial advertising. Nam is a self-taught illustrator who credits artists such as Burne Hogarth, Jim Lee and Masamune Shiro for shaping his artistic style and vision. He has worked for Nike, ToykoPop, Radical Publishing and Image Comics where he illustrated the critically acclaimed *Samurai's Blood*.

GARRY LEACH—INKER

is a British artist best known for his work co-creating the new *Marvelman* with writer Alan Moore. As an artist Garry was a frequent contributor to *2000AD* working on *Dan Dare*, *Judge Dredd*, *The V.C.s* and *Future Shocks*. At DC Comics Garry worked on *Legion of Superheroes*, *Hit Man*, *Monarchy* and *Global Frequency*, while over at Marvel Comics, he inked Chris Weston on *The Twelve*. Garry has been a cover artist for Marvel, DC, *2000AD*, *Eclipse*, *Dynamic Forces*, and Kellogg's Corn Flakes.

FAHRIZA KAMAPUTRA–COLORIST

was born and raised in southern Jakarta. In 2010 he worked as colorist on a local comic book *Vienetta and the Stupid Aliens* which led to his work on the web comic *Rokki* and Madeleine Holly-Rosling's *Boston Metaphysical Society* with the studio STELLAR LABS. Fahriza now works as a freelance artist.

DAVE ELLIOTT–EDITOR

has worked on such diverse titles as *A1*, *Deadline*, *Viz*, *Heavy Metal*, *2000AD*, *Justice League of America*, *Transformers*, *GI Joe*, *The Real Ghostbusters* and *Doctor Who*. Dave co-founded Radical Studios where he oversaw the development and launch of Radical's premiere comic book titles several of which were sold as film properties including *Hercules*, *Freedom Formula* and *Oblivion*. He recently launched the graphic novel series *Odyssey* and *The Weirding Willows* with Titan Comics.

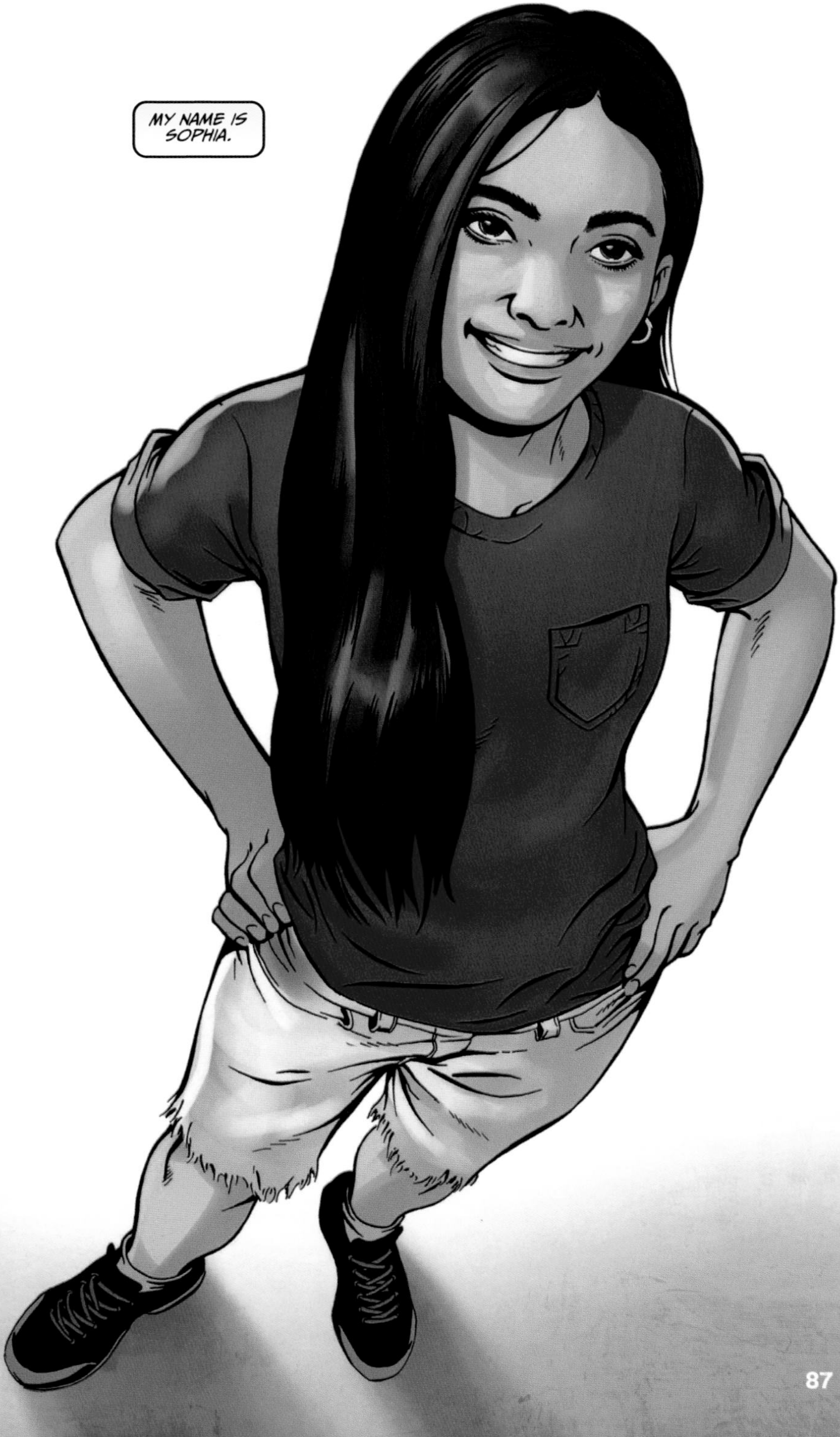
MY NAME IS SOPHIA.

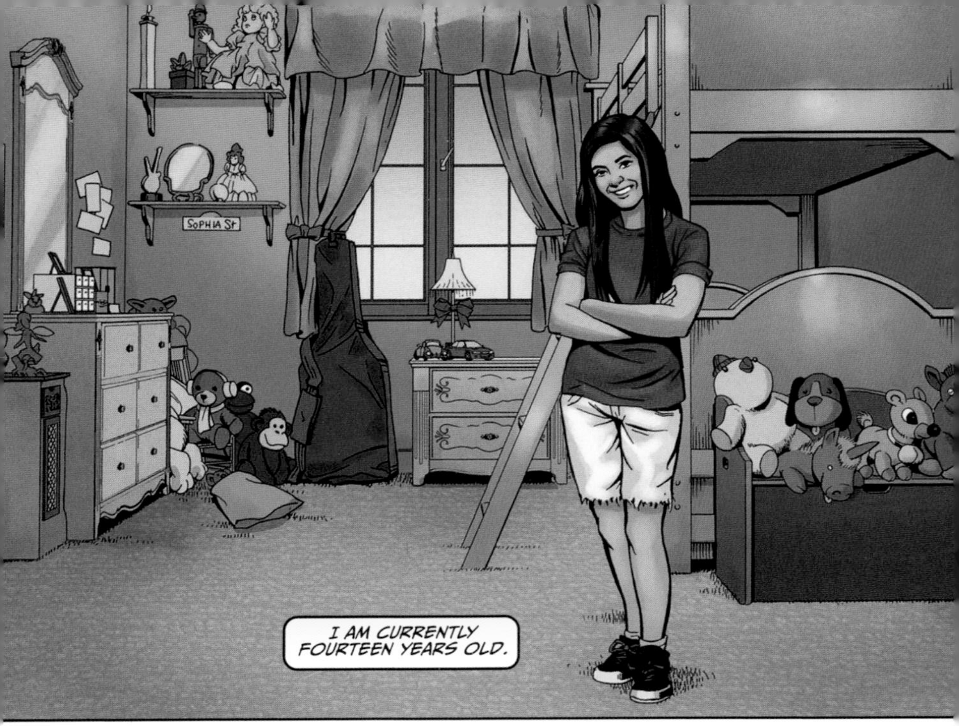
SOPHIA St
I AM CURRENTLY FOURTEEN YEARS OLD.

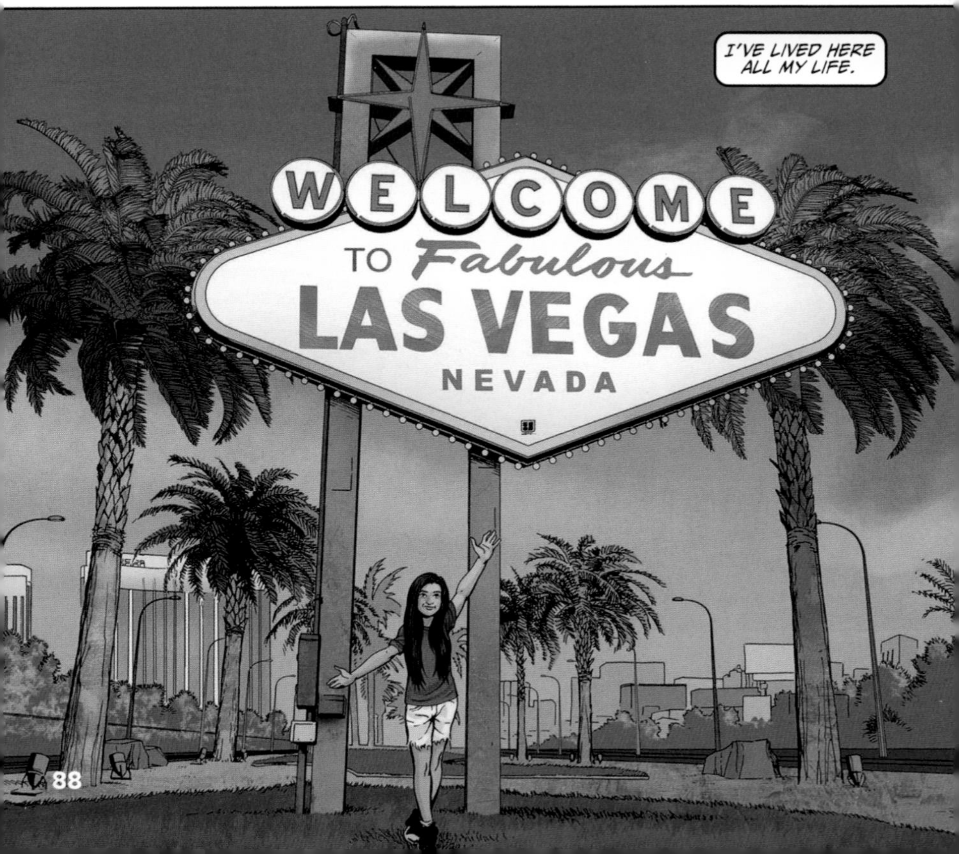
I'VE LIVED HERE ALL MY LIFE.
WELCOME
TO Fabulous
LAS VEGAS
NEVADA

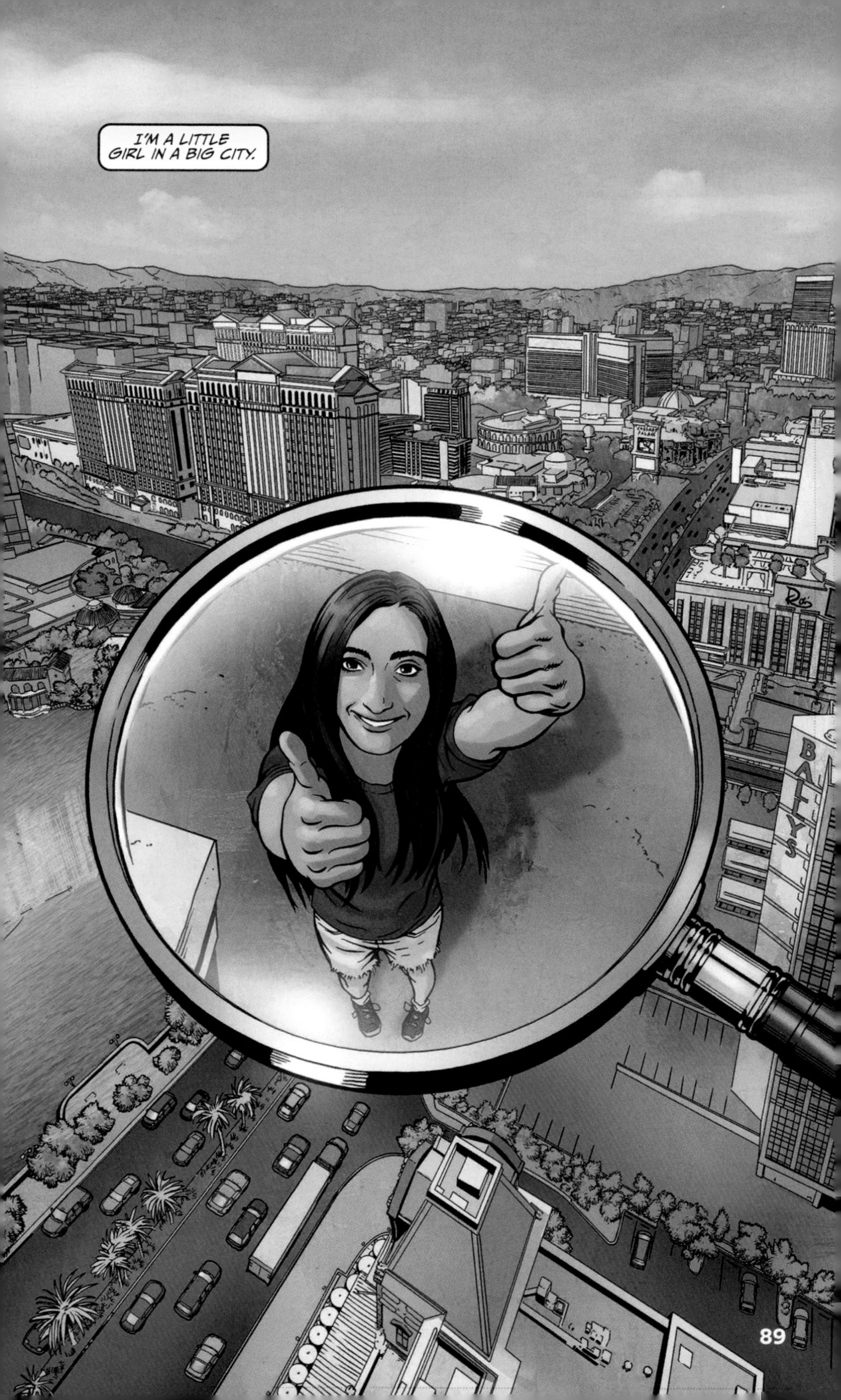
I'M A LITTLE GIRL IN A BIG CITY.
BALLYS

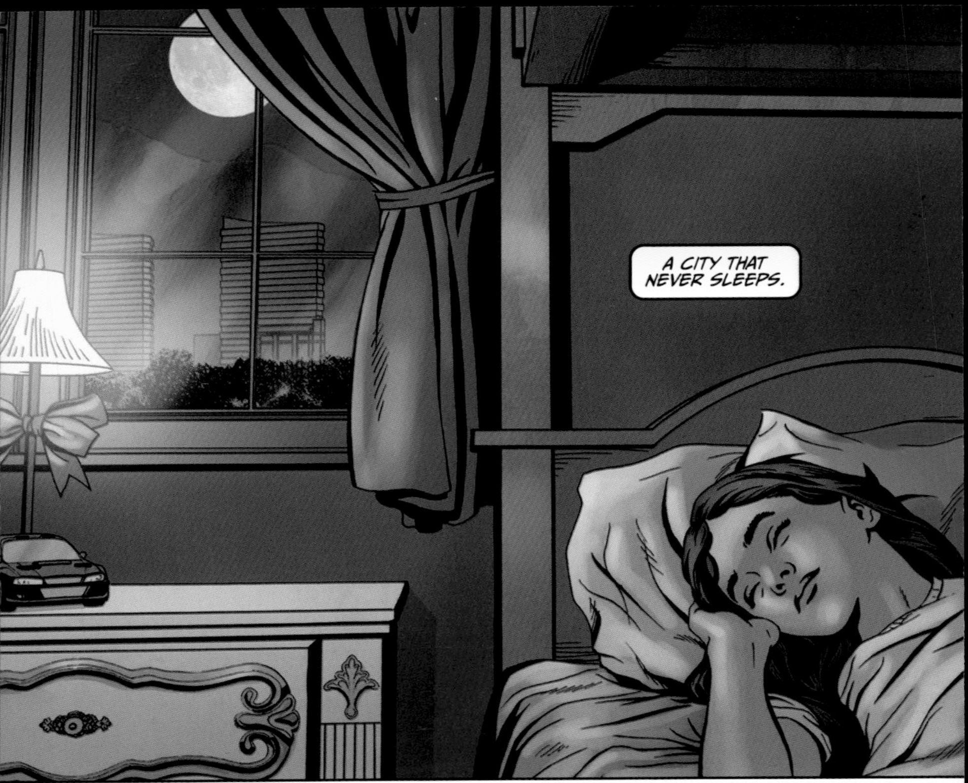
A CITY THAT
NEVER SLEEPS.

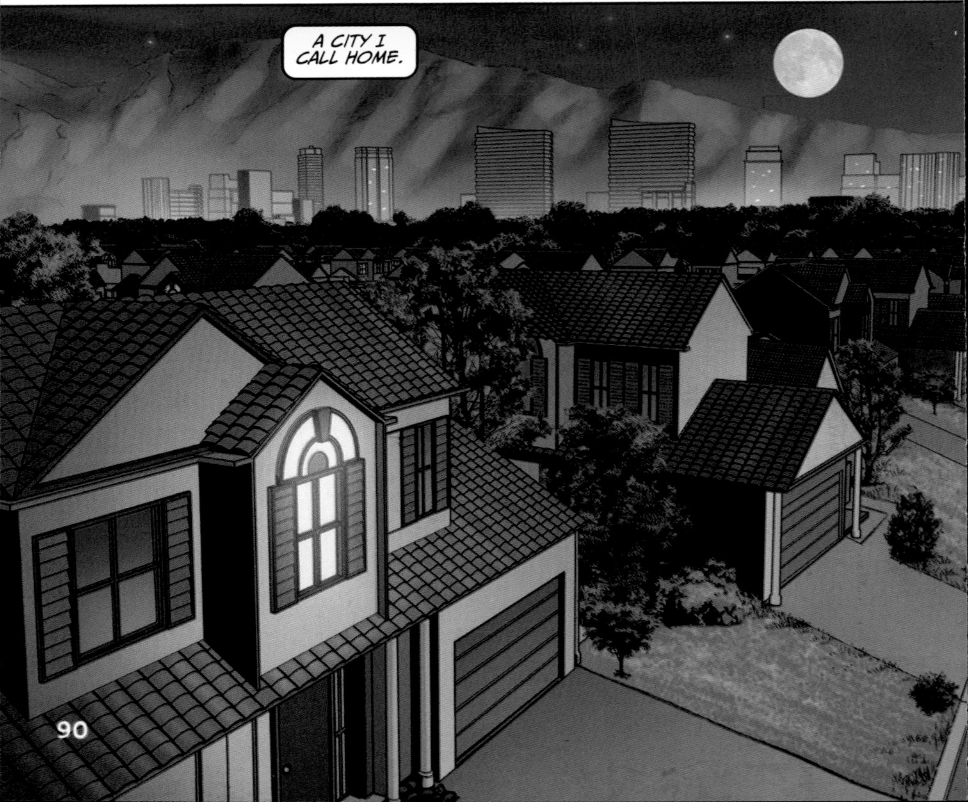
A CITY I
CALL HOME.

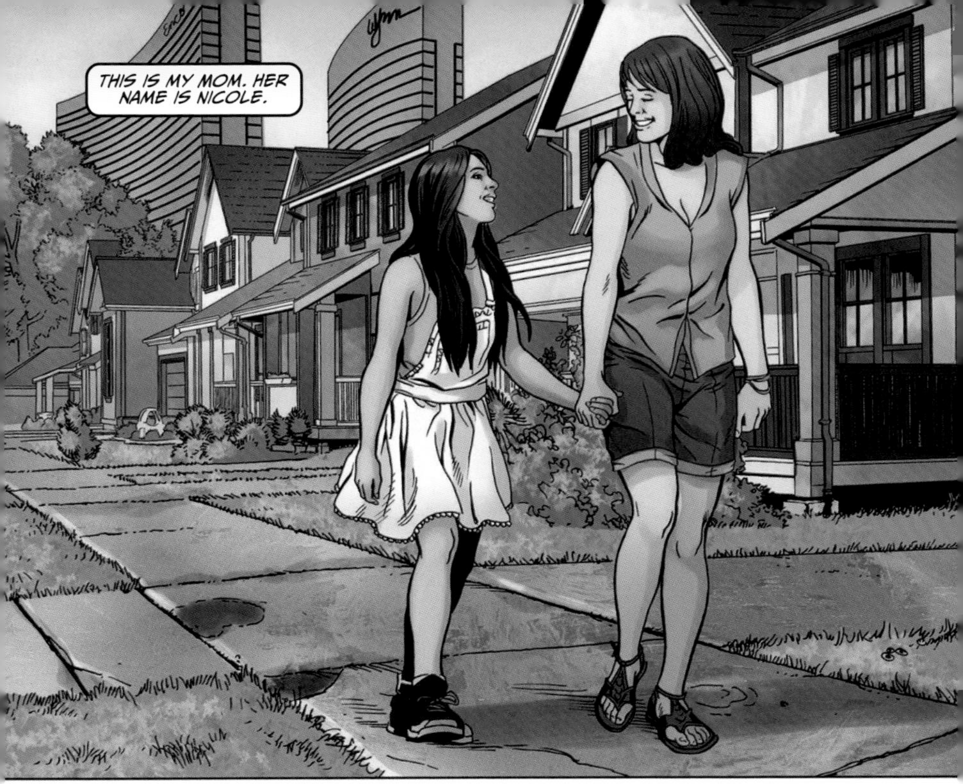
THIS IS MY MOM. HER NAME IS NICOLE.

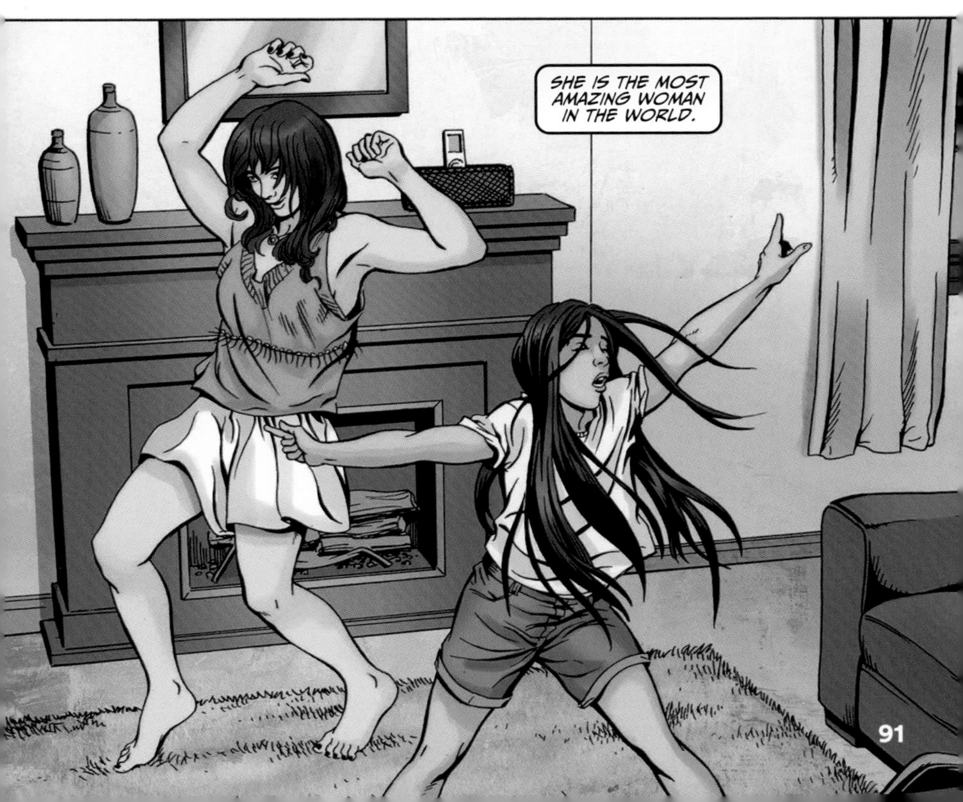
SHE IS THE MOST AMAZING WOMAN IN THE WORLD.

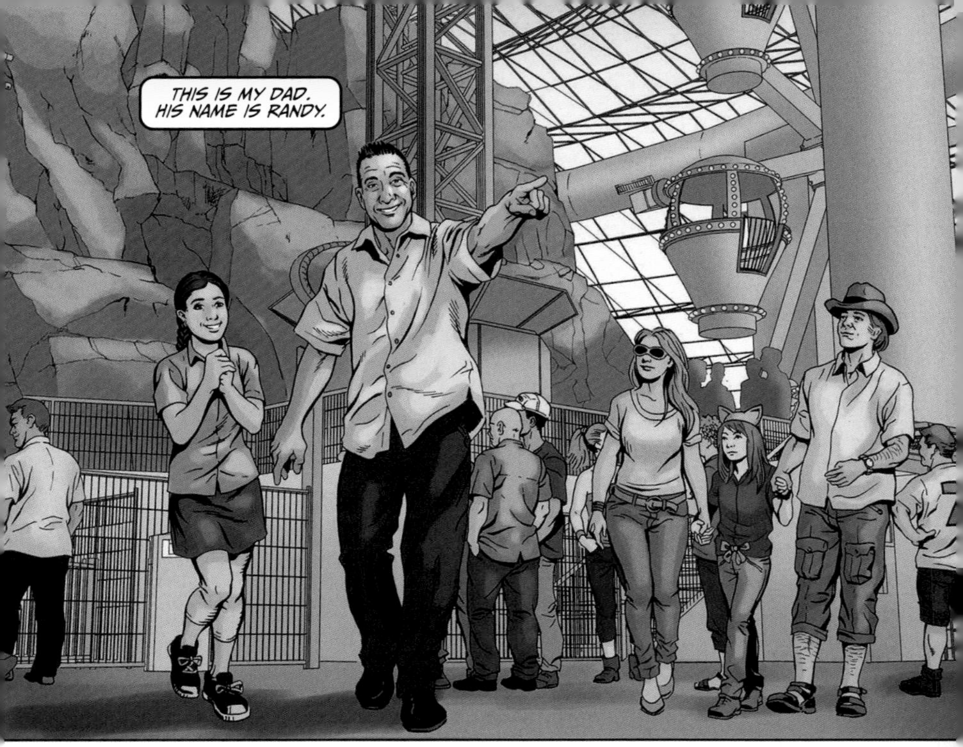
THIS IS MY DAD.
HIS NAME IS RANDY.

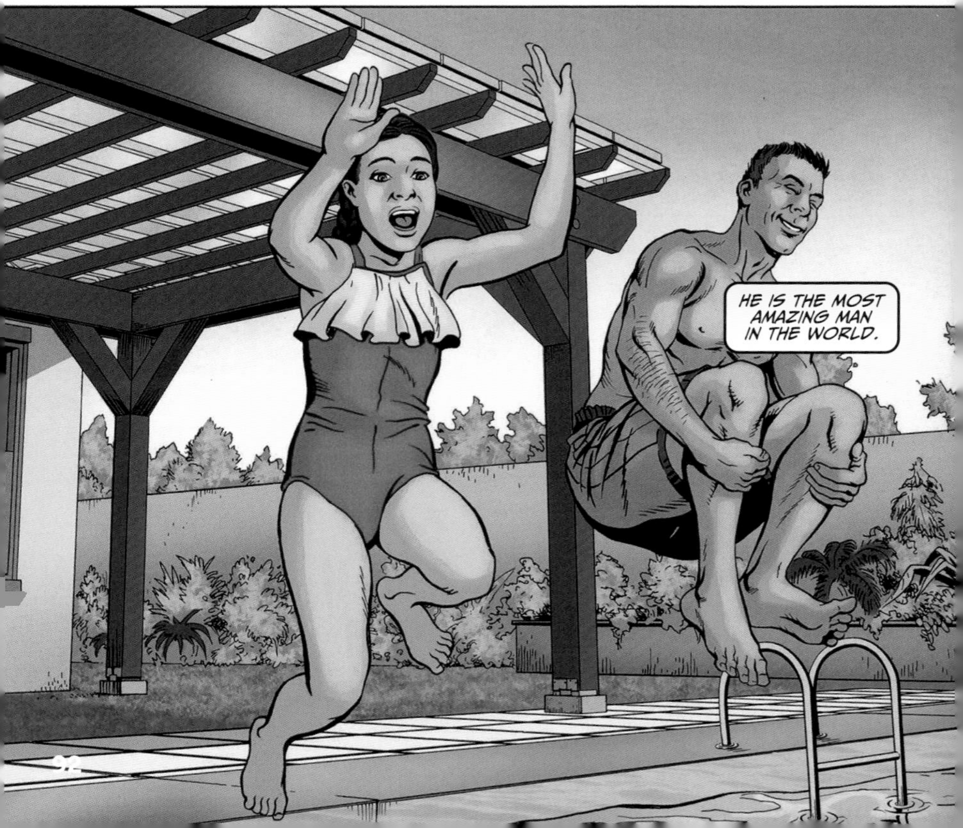
HE IS THE MOST
AMAZING MAN
IN THE WORLD.

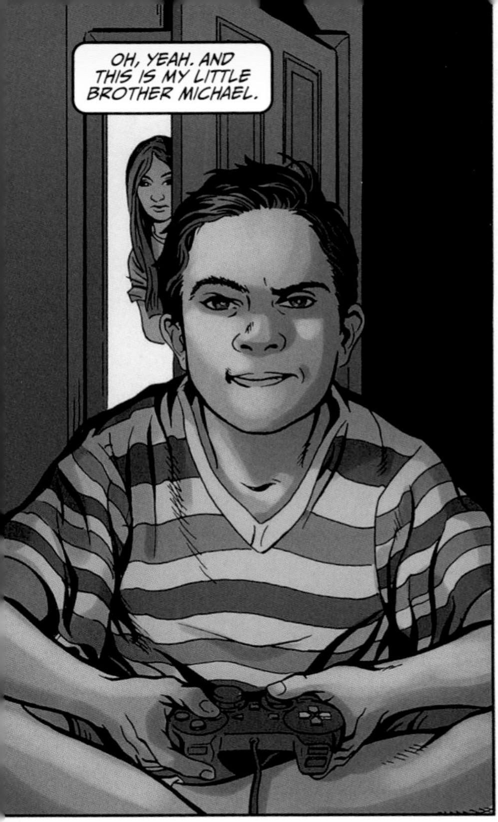
OH, YEAH. AND THIS IS MY LITTLE BROTHER MICHAEL.

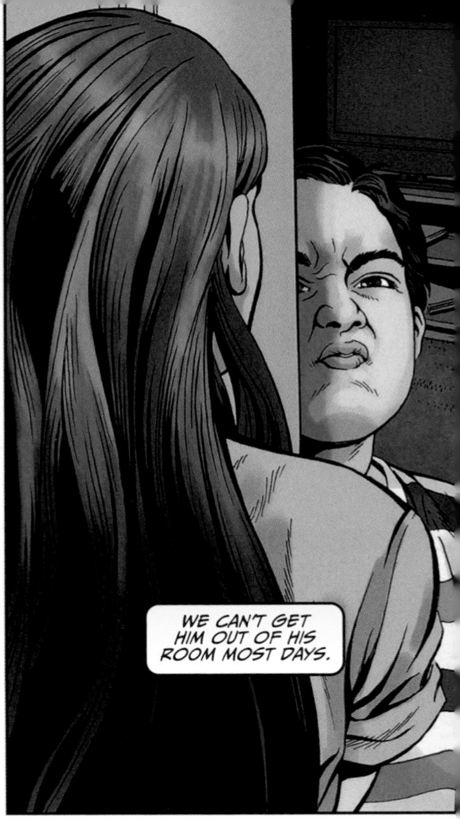
WE CAN'T GET HIM OUT OF HIS ROOM MOST DAYS.

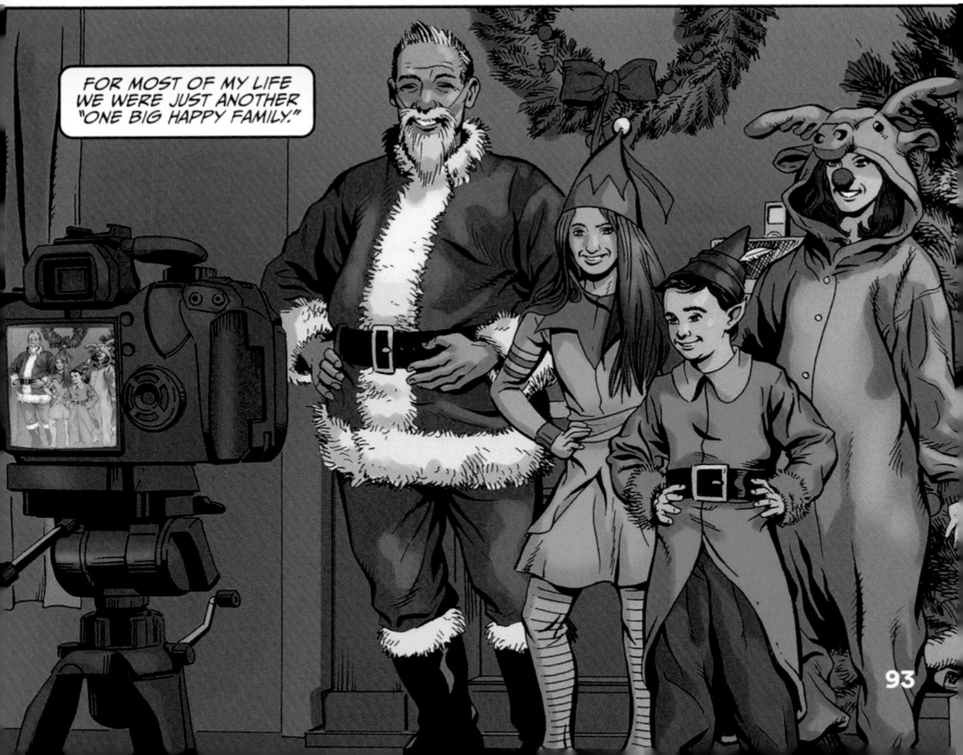
FOR MOST OF MY LIFE WE WERE JUST ANOTHER "ONE BIG HAPPY FAMILY."

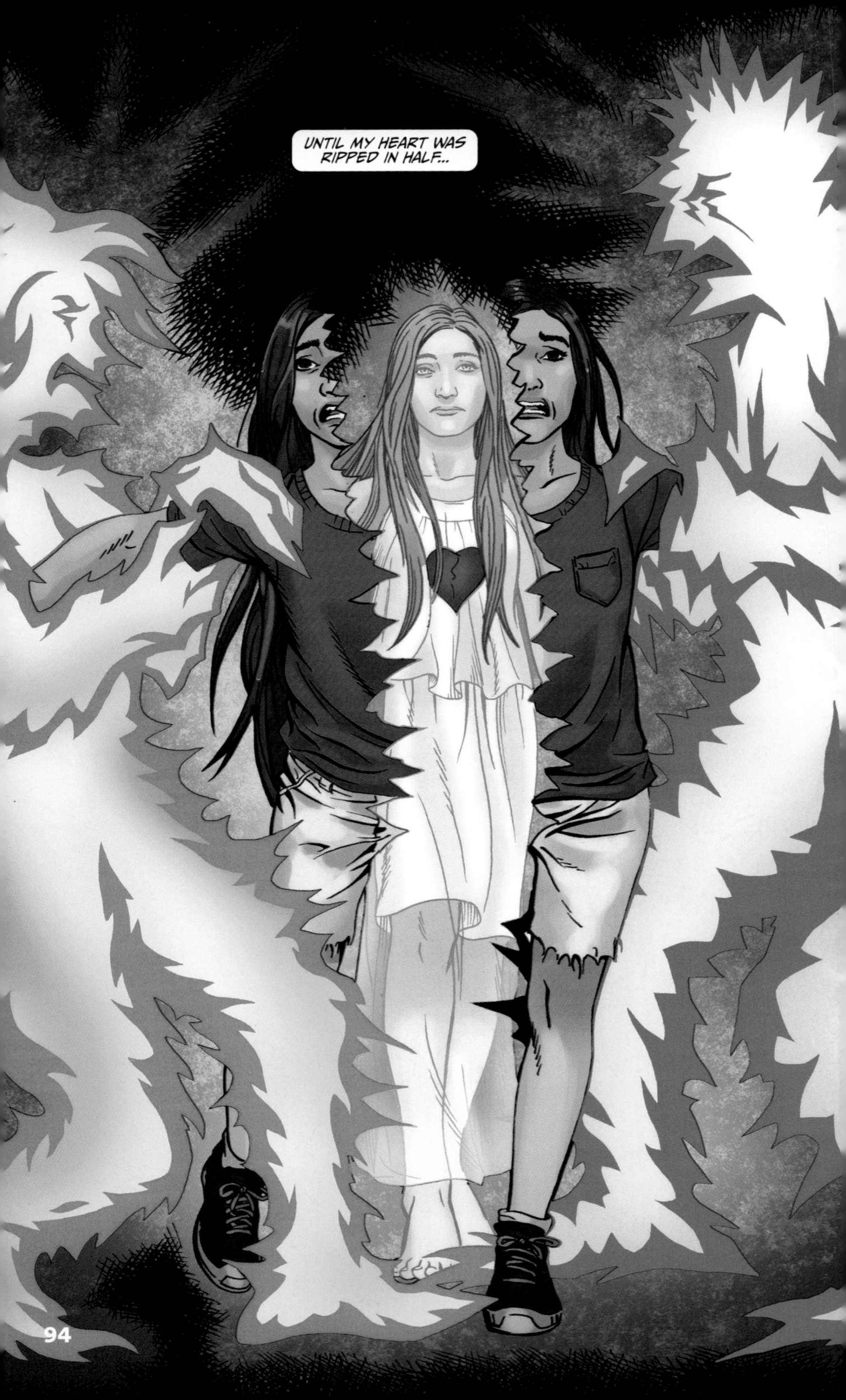
UNTIL MY HEART WAS RIPPED IN HALF...

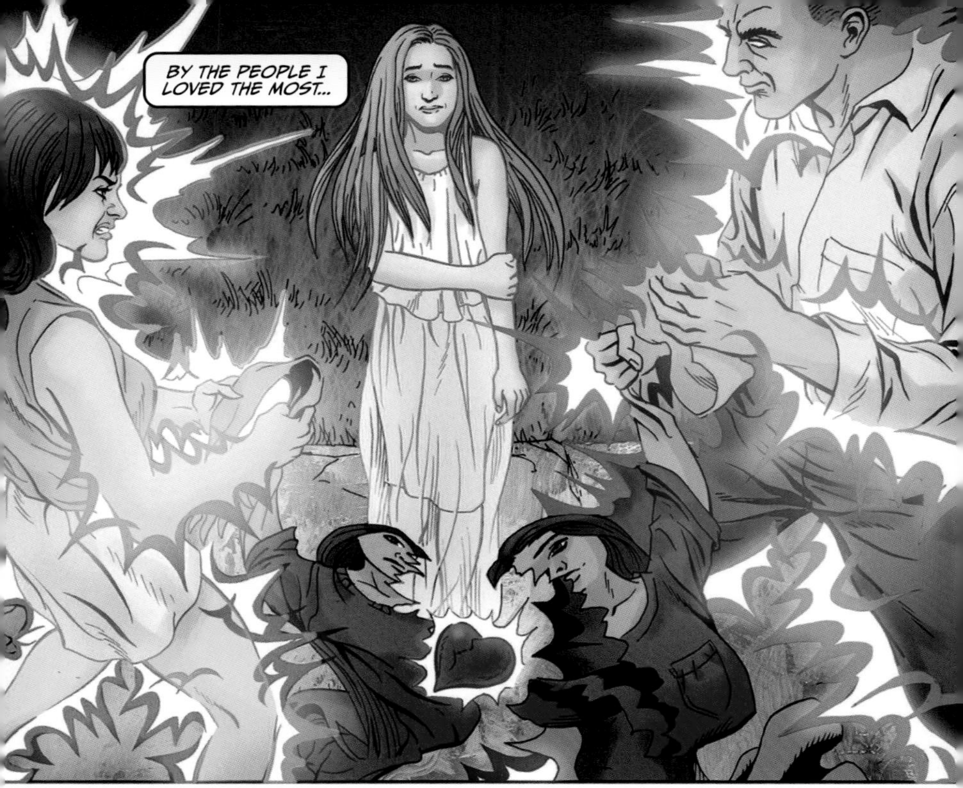
BY THE PEOPLE I LOVED THE MOST...

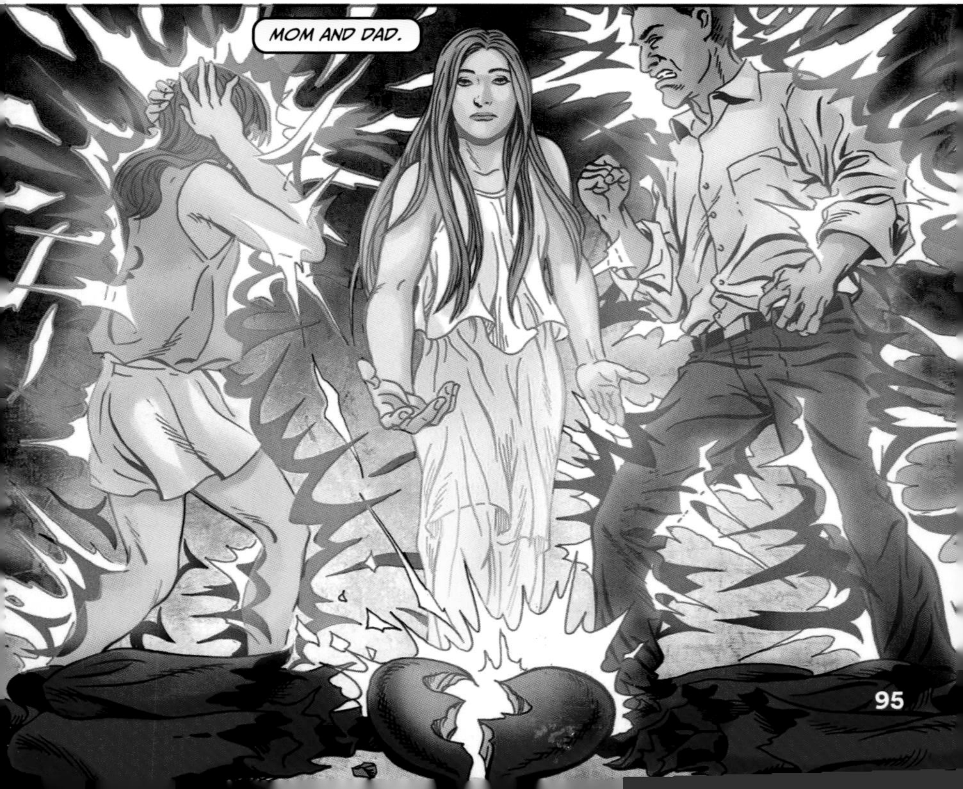
MOM AND DAD.

NEW FOR FALL 2018

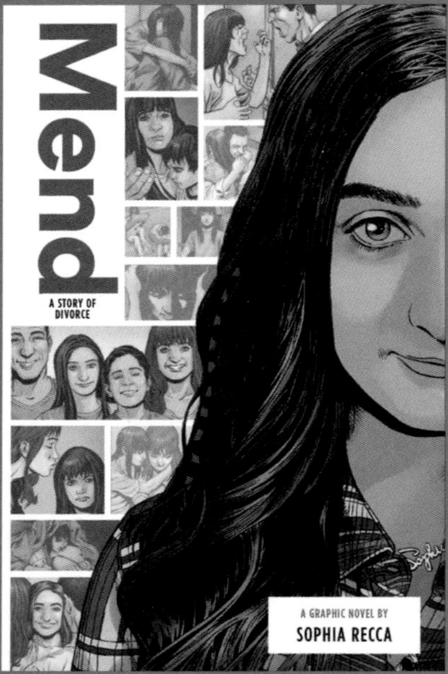
Mend
A STORY OF DIVORCE
A GRAPHIC NOVEL BY
SOPHIA RECCA

MEND: A STORY OF DIVORCE

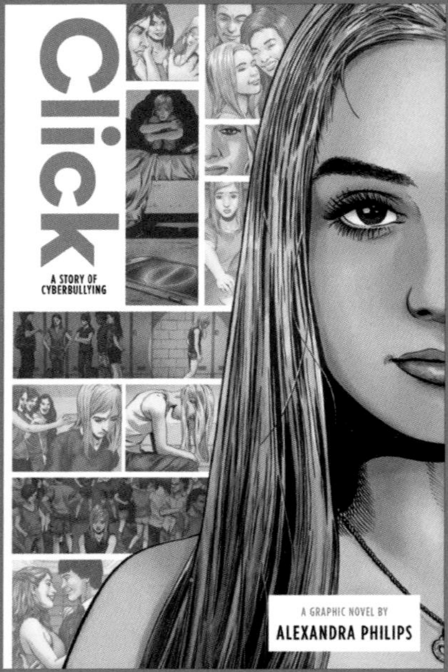
Click
A STORY OF CYBERBULLYING
A GRAPHIC NOVEL BY
ALEXANDRA PHILIPS

CLICK: A STORY OF CYBERBULLYING

COMING SPRING 2019

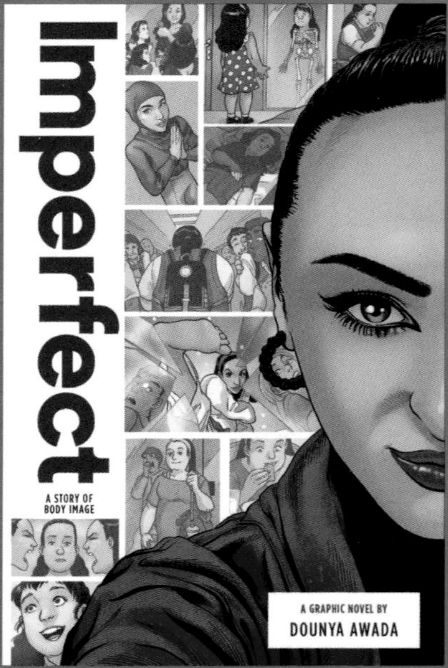
Imperfect
A STORY OF BODY IMAGE
A GRAPHIC NOVEL BY
DOUNYA AWADA

IMPERFECT: A STORY OF BODY IMAGE

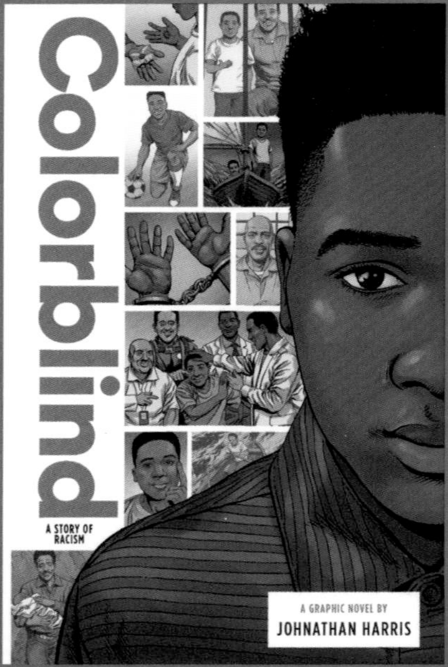
Colorblind
A STORY OF RACISM
A GRAPHIC NOVEL BY
JOHNATHAN HARRIS

COLORBLIND: A STORY OF RACISM